the photographer's
guide to
Canyon Country

Where to Find Perfect Shots and How to Take Them

John Annerino

THE COUNTRYMAN PRESS
WOODSTOCK, VERMONT

In memory of expedition and pioneer photographers
Timothy H. O'Sullivan, E. O. Beaman, James Fennemore, John K. Hillers,
William H. Jackson, and Charles F. Lummis. They got here first.

Special thanks to Jennifer Thompson, Dale Gelfand, Clare Innes,
Susan Livingston, and Paul Woodward.

Text and photographs copyright © 2006 by John Annerino

First Edition

Library of Congress Cataloging-in-Publication Data has been applied for.

ISBN 0-88150-663-X

Cover photograph of Park Avenue, Arches National Park, and interior photographs © John Annerino
Cover and interior design by Susan Livingston
Map by Paul Woodward, © The Countryman Press

Published by The Countryman Press, P.O. Box 748, Woodstock, VT 05091
Distributed by W.W. Norton & Company, Inc. 500 Fifth Avenue, New York, NY 10110

Printed in Spain by Artes Graficas Toledo

10 9 8 7 6 5 4 3 2 1

Title page: Zion National Park from Scenic Road

**Also by
John Annerino**

Photography

CANYON COUNTRY:
A Photographic Journey

GRAND CANYON WILD:
A Photographic Journey

ROUGHSTOCK:
The Toughest Events in Rodeo

APACHE:
The Sacred Path to Womanhood

PEOPLE OF LEGEND:
Native Americans of the Southwest

THE WILD COUNTRY OF MEXICO
La tierra salvaje de México

CANYONS OF THE SOUTHWEST

HIGH RISK PHOTOGRAPHY:
The Adventure Behind the Image

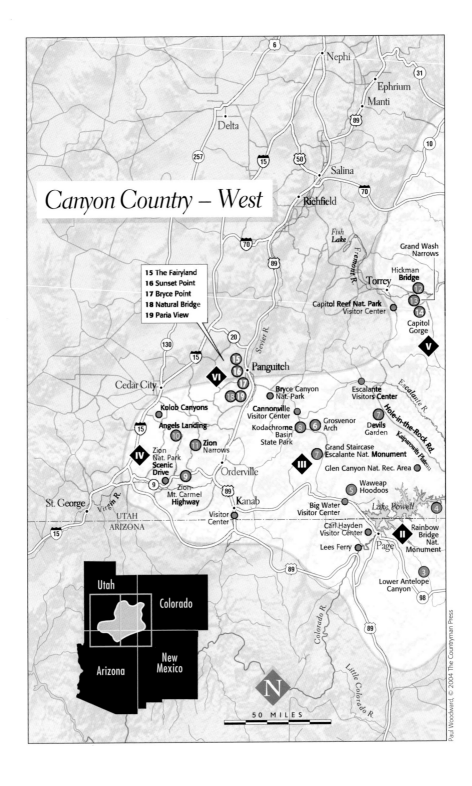

Canyon Country – West

6

31

Nephi

Ephrium

Manti

89

Delta

10

257

15

50

Salina

70

130

70

Fish *Lake*

Richfield

89

Grand Wash Narrows

Hickman **Bridge** 12

Torrey 13

Capitol Reef Nat. Park
Visitor Center 14

Capitol Gorge

V

15 The Fairyland
16 Sunset Point
17 Bryce Point
18 Natural Bridge
19 Paria View

20

Sevier R.

15 The Fairyland
16 Sunset Point

15

16 Panguitch

Cedar City

VI

17

18 19

Kolob Canyons

Escalante Visitors Center

Bryce Canyon Nat. Park

Cannonville Visitor Center

Kodachrome Basin State Park

8 6 Grosvenor Arch

Escalante R.

Hole-in-the-Rock Rd.

7 Devils Garden

Kaiparowits Plateau

Angels Landing

15

10

11 **Zion Narrows**

IV

Zion Nat. Park
Scenic Drive

9

9 Zion-
Mt. Carmel
Highway

Orderville

Grand Staircase
Escalante Nat. **Monument** 7

Glen Canyon Nat. Rec. Area

III

St. George

Virgin R.

UTAH
ARIZONA

89

Kanab

Waweap Hoodoos 5

Big Water
Visitor Center

Visitor Center

Lake Powell

4

15

Carl Hayden
Visitor Center

Lees Ferry

II Rainbow
Bridge
Nat.
Monument

Page

89

Colorado R.

Lower Antelope
Canyon 3

98

89

Little Colorado R.

Utah

Colorado

Arizona

New
Mexico

N

50 MILES

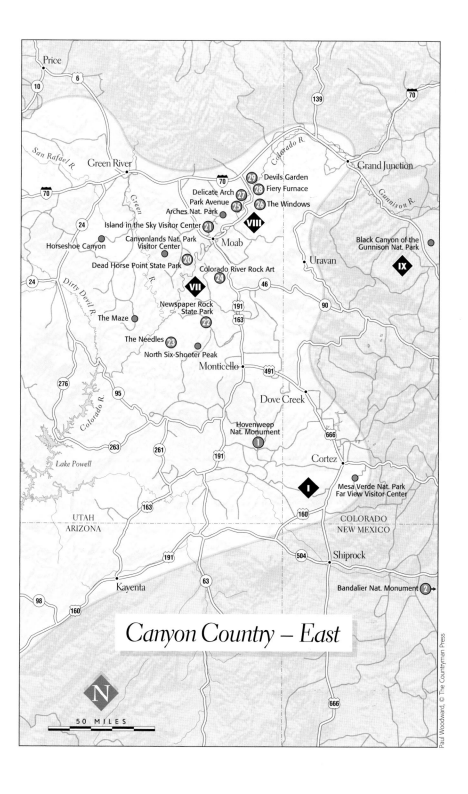

Price

10

6

70

139

70

San Rafael R.

Green River

Colorado R.

Grand Junction

70

Green

70

29 Devils Garden

28 Fiery Furnace

Delicate Arch 27

Park Avenue

25

26 The Windows

Arches Nat. Park

VIII

Gunnison R.

24

Island in the Sky Visitor Center 21

Horseshoe Canyon

Canyonlands Nat. Park
Visitor Center

Moab

Black Canyon of the
Gunnison Nat. Park

24

Dirty Devil R.

Dead Horse Point State Park

20

Colorado River Rock Art

Uravan

IX

24

R.

VII

24

46

Newspaper Rock
State Park

191

90

The Maze

163

The Needles

23

22

North Six-Shooter Peak

Monticello

491

276

95

Dove Creek

Colorado R.

Hovenweep
Nat. Monument

666

263

261

191

1

Cortez

Lake Powell

I

Mesa Verde Nat. Park
Far View Visitor Center

163

160

UTAH
ARIZONA

COLORADO
NEW MEXICO

191

504

Shiprock

98

160

63

Kayenta

Bandalier Nat. Monument 2

Canyon Country – East

666

N

50 MILES

Cliff Palace, Mesa Verde National Park

Contents

Map of Canyon Country 4
Introduction 8

I. Mesa Verde National Park 16
1. Hovenweep National Monument . . 19
2. Bandelier National Monument 21

II. Glen Canyon National Recreation Area 24
3. Lower Antelope Canyon 27
4. Rainbow Bridge National Monument/Navajo Mountain Lodge Site 29

III. Grand Staircase–Escalante National Monument 32
5. Wahweap Hoodoos 35
6. Grosvenor Arch 36
7. Devils Garden 38
8. Kodachrome Basin State Park 40

IV. Zion National Park 42
Zion Canyon Scenic Drive 42
9. Zion–Mt. Carmel Highway 46
10. Angels Landing 47
11. Zion Narrows 48

V. Capitol Reef National Park 51
12. Hickman Bridge 55
13. Grand Wash Narrows 55
14. Capitol Gorge 57

VI. Bryce Canyon National Park . . . 58
15. The Fairyland 61
16. Sunset Point 63
17. Bryce Point 65
18. Natural Bridge 66
19. Paria View 66

VII. Canyonlands National Park 68
20. Dead Horse Point State Park 69
21. Island in the Sky 72
22. Newspaper Rock State Park 75
23. The Needles 77
24. Colorado River Rock Art 78

VIII. Arches National Park 80
25. Park Avenue & Courthouse Towers 83
26. The Windows 84
27. Delicate Arch 86
28. Fiery Furnace 87
29. Devils Garden 88

IX. Black Canyon of the Gunnison National Park 89

Suggested Reading 92
Trip & Expedition Planner 94

Sand Dune Arch, Arches National Park

Introduction

Stand at the foot of Yosemite National Park's El Capitan, Yellowstone National Park's Old Faithful, or Rocky Mountain National Park's Longs Peak, and you'll understand why these western landmarks are national treasures. Run the Green and Colorado Rivers through Canyonlands National Park, thread the narrow fissures of Grand Staircase–Escalante National Monument, or gaze in wonder at Delicate Arch in Arches National Park, and you will also understand why these majestic landscapes became American icons. But you will be dwarfed in a wilderness of stone that runs to the horizon in every direction. You can see that from the sacred summit of Navajo Mountain. You can see that from the eastern rim of Bryce Canyon National Park's Paunsaugunt Plateau. And you can see that as you drive from the sub-Alpine forests of Boulder Mountain into the desert ramparts of Capitol Reef National Park's Waterpocket Fold. Even from such lofty vantages, it is difficult to see—or photograph—Canyon Country from any one viewpoint. For good reason.

Encompassing 130,000 square miles of Utah, Arizona, Colorado, and New Mexico, the 6,000-foot-high Colorado Plateau is the second largest plateau on earth, and it forms one of the most spectacular regions in the world. Through wind, water, erosion, and the ancient upheaval of great land masses, the Colorado and Green Rivers and their myriad tributaries have sculpted towering spires, soaring arches, vaulted mesas, tundra-covered mountains, and slickrock canyons. Home to an ancient people who built magnifi-

cent cliff dwellings that still stand ages later, the cultural history, geography, and geology of the Colorado Plateau is so extraordinary among the earth's natural wonders that the entire region was nominated a UNESCO World Heritage Site.

Characterized by blood-red mesas, terra-cotta cliffs and terraces, dark and narrow canyons illuminated with heavenly shafts of light, and the mystical mountains of Native peoples, few places on earth rival the astonishing grandeur and beauty of Canyon Country. Few places in North America drew more attention from pioneer and expedition photographers than Canyon Country. And few places in the West have captivated the focus of today's photographers more than Canyon Country.

First Photographers

Native Americans were the first to recognize that an image could be captured and reflected, if only fleetingly, on the surface of the water. As people went about their daily task of collecting drinking water, they could see the details of their eyes and faces in still pools of water, the green leaves of a cottonwood tree fluttering behind them, the white cliffs of Navajo Sandstone towering overhead. Observing pioneer photographers at work throughout Canyon Country during the late 1800s, the Native peoples gave them names that reflected their own experiences of taking mental photographs. The Ute called John K. Hillers "Myself in the Water," and the Mojave called Timothy H. O'Sullivan "Shadow Catcher."

Pioneer and Expedition Photographers

A handful of pioneer and expedition photographers were the first to photograph the national parks and monuments featured in this book. In fact, the notoriety and acclaim that traveling exhibitions of their images generated often led to presidential proclamations of official park or monument status. Together or independent of one another, these photographers braved wild white-water rapids in handmade wooden boats, used hemp ropes to haul heavy wooden cameras and tripods up imposing cliff faces, and traced deep, haunting canyons on foot and pack string. Before all was said and done, they mapped and photographed the last explored region in the contiguous United States; discovered rivers, mountains, and cliff dwellings; and named geographical features whose original names were lost to Native American oral traditions. The diaries they kept told of grueling hardships and glorious wonders that few readers—then or now—could have imagined or endured. And perhaps best of all, they made an extraordinary visual record of the rugged land and its resilient people.

Their rudimentary tools were heavy, unwieldy, and fragile and included wooden box cameras, (5x8, 11x14, and 20x24 formats), spike-tipped tripods, glass collodion wet plates, toxic chemicals, metal mixing trays, and canvas dark tents. Weighing from several hundred pounds to a ton, their gear was hauled by mule-driven wooden ambulances turned rolling darkrooms, in leaky wooden boats, on the backs of pack mules, or strapped to their own shoulders as they traversed the most rugged and beautiful terrain they'd ever seen. As proof of their hard-won efforts, they brought back images that still make modern viewers ask, "How did they *get* that picture?!" The answer: Most often, through weeks of toil and deprivation. In comparison, whether we travel by foot, raft, rope, pickup, four-wheel-drive SUV, or shuttle bus, we've got it easy.

The following are some of the premier pioneer photographers. Some became giants. Others faded from history. All remain an inspiration for modern landscape, wilderness, and adventure photographers.

Timothy O'Sullivan: A Civil War photographer who shot graphic images of one of the nation's most gruesome wars, Timothy O'Sullivan cut his teeth on the blood-stained battlefields of Gettysburg for Brady's Photographic Corps. At war's end, many Civil War photographers like O'Sullivan headed west to record the daunting landscape and its unfolding history. O'Sullivan was one of the first. Among many adventures, O'Sullivan photographed perilous expeditions that took him from Panama's Darian Gap to Nevada's Carson Desert. Attached to the 1871 Wheeler Survey, O'Sullivan spent a month photographing the wild canyon scenery that the Mojave Indians guided the expedition through, as members struggled to paddle and portage 160 miles *up* the Colorado River from Black Canyon to Diamond Creek in what became Grand Canyon National Park.

E. O. Beaman: Another Civil War veteran, E. O. Beaman traveled to New York and became a professional photographer. While Major John Wesley Powell was buying photographic equipment for his second expedition down the Green and Colorado Rivers in 1871-72, Beaman was recommended to Powell by the E & H T Anthony Company. Beaman ran the upper half of the Powell expedition from Green River, Wyoming, to Lees Ferry, Arizona, becoming the first to photograph Labyrinth, Stillwater, and Cataract Canyons in what became Canyonlands National Park and Glen Canyon National Recreation Area.

James Fennemore: In the fall of 1871, Powell traveled to Salt Lake City to have prints made from 250 of Beaman's stereoscopic negatives. The work was done by James Fennemore at the Charles R. Savage gallery. When Beaman left Powell's service to strike out on his own in the winter of 1872, Powell hired Fennemore to replace him. During his brief tenure with Powell between March 19 and July 19, 1872, Fennemore produced 70 negatives while photographing the expedition as it journeyed overland through the terra incognita of the Colorado Plateau in search of the Dirty Devil River. Fennemore and his assistant, John K. Hillers, took the first-known photographs of what became Zion, Bryce Canyon, and Capitol Reef National Parks as well as Grand Staircase–Escalante National Monument. Some historians believe Fennemore's greatest contribution was teaching photography to Hillers, who replaced his mentor when he became ill. But Fennemore remains notable to this day for the haunting photograph he took of John D. Lee sitting on his coffin wearing a top hat before he was executed by a firing squad for his alleged role in the Mountain Meadows Massacre.

John K. "Jack" Hillers: A German immigrant, New York Naval Brigade member, and Salt Lake City teamster, John K. Hillers was hired by Powell to work as a boat-man on the second Colorado River Expedition in 1871–72. After Hillers took over Fennemore's responsibilities, he photographed the lower half of the Colorado River expedition and between August 17 and September 9, 1872, became the first to photograph the length of the Grand Canyon from Lees Ferry to Kanab Creek. Hillers's unprecedented work did not eclipse the fact that Timothy H. O'Sullivan had earned the honors of taking the first-known photographs of the Grand Canyon on October 19, 1871. Hillers went on to take over three thousand photographs, many of them memorable ethnographic portraits of the Paiute and Ute. As a result of Hillers's work with Powell, he became chief photographer for the U.S. Geological Survey.

William Henry Jackson: A Civil War artist turned photographer, William Jackson went West and became a giant of American landscape photography, capturing the nation's crown jewels from Yellowstone to the Grand Canyon. Attached to the 1874 Hayden Survey of Colorado, Jackson and two assistants hauled a hundred pounds of photo equipment on their backs—including an 11x14 wet-plate camera—to the summit of 13,224-foot Notch Mountain to take the first-known photograph of Colorado's mysterious 14,005-foot Mount of the Holy Cross. Veering from the Hayden Survey to explore ancestral Puebloan ruins, Jackson also took the first-known photographs of what became Mesa Verde National Park and Hovenweep National Monument.

Charles F. Lummis: As tough and independent a lot as pioneer photographers were, few could match the grit and stamina of Charles F. Lummis. During 1884,

Lummis walked 3,507 miles from Cincinnati, Ohio, to Los Angeles, California, to take a job as editor for the *Los Angeles Times*. En route, Lummis broke his arm while chasing a deer in Arizona's Painted Desert. Lummis reduced the bloody compound fracture himself, climbed a Grand Canyon peak with his dog, and completed his transcontinental walk. After leaving his post at the *Los Angeles Times*, Lummis photographed Adolf F. Bandelier's archaeological and ethnographic survey of New Mexico's Pajarito Plateau, taking some of the first-known photographs of what became Bandelier National Monument.

Ellsworth and Emery Kolb: Pennsylvania-born Ellsworth and Emery Kolb went west in 1901 and staked out their photographic claim of the Grand Canyon. They became legendary canyon explorers and photographers, becoming famous for taking the first motion pictures of their kind of their 1911 Colorado River expedition from Green River, Wyoming, through the Grand Canyon to the Gulf of California. (See *The Photographer's Guide to the Grand Canyon*.)

Tabula Rasa

At the time that these pioneer and expedition photographers went West, the visual slate was clean and they could interpret the landscape as they saw it. When Timothy O'Sullivan drove his mule-powered darkroom wagon into the drifting sands of the Nevada desert in 1867, there were no other images that could influence how he might photograph the forlorn desolation of the Carson Desert. That no longer holds true for today's photographers.

Landscape, Wilderness, and Adventure Photography

People pick up a camera to freeze a moment in time for myriad reasons. Before packing for your trip and heading into Canyon Country, determine what your goals are so you can make the most of your time, money, and efforts. Do you want to capture mementos from a summer vacation to e-mail friends, family, or someone else dear to you? Are you an amateur or student photographer with aspirations of building a foundation of experience, knowledge, and bank of images that lead to becoming a professional? Are you a landscape painter in need of a visual reference or a geology professor requiring illustrations for a PowerPoint presentation? Are you an adventurer hoping to record an expedition for posterity, the historical record, or a magazine essay? Are you an author set on illustrating a nonfiction book of your wilderness journey? Are you a stock shooter who's aspiring to photograph the great icons of the American West? Are you a calendar photographer in quest of 13 images that say "this is Arches National Park"? Are you a photo essayist shooting a photography book?

However you may answer those questions, I have a simple rule of thumb: "Shoot wide, and zero in." Years after I finally broke into *Life* magazine I used to carry a notecard in my camera bag listing the eight different kinds of photographs *Life* picture editors wanted to see before a photo essay had a chance of making it into the book: 1. Introductory or overall shot, 2. Medium shot, 3. Close-up shot, 4. Portrait, 5. Interaction shot, 6. Signature shot, 7. Sequence of shots, and 8. Closing shot. By the time I hit my stride professionally, most American magazines no longer devoted the kind of space that photo essays required. So I sought other venues until I found wide success publishing photo essays in glossy European, Asian, and Latin American magazines. Those experiences gave me the confidence to make the leap into photography books.

I continue to shoot wide and zero in for scenic photography, often incorporating the first three kinds of shots from the *Life* formula. If you're a landscape photographer, establish the overall scene or scenes; then focus on supporting scenes and details. For example, if you're going to photograph Arches National Park, what's the one photograph that says Arches to you: Delicate Arch framing a moonrise at twilight? Turret Arch viewed through the North Window at sunrise? Landscape Arch at dawn? What are the supporting scenes: The pink fins of Devils Garden at sunset? A shaft of light illuminating the gloomy depths of the Fiery Furnace? What are the details: The bark of an alligator juniper tree? A collared lizard? The texture of fossilized sandstone? Just as importantly ask yourself this: Have I seen this picture before?

Photographing Canyon Country

Vision: Many national park and monument viewpoints have been photographed so often by so many different photographers that it's difficult to take an original composition if you're determined to "improve upon," or photocopy, a popular landmark from the same distance, angle, or point of view. Carefully consider how your photograph will be different and bet-ter than the racks of postcard images you'll see at every national park and monument. Change the framing, perspective, natural light, and viewpoint until you discover something new and exciting in your viewfinder.

The first time I went to photograph Delicate Arch for one of my early photography books, I saw dozens of amateur and professional photographers lined up on the same perch waiting to take the same sunset view of Delicate Arch with the 12,721-foot La Sal Mountains in the background. I remembered something I'd learned earlier: If the pack is crowded together in the same spot taking the same photograph, look for a different but no less compelling point of view. I looked across the bay from the crowded ledge and viewed a lone promontory southwest of Delicate Arch. I scrambled up it and, even before I looked through the viewfinder, I saw photographs that would stand apart from the others being taken that day. Listen to your heart and what speaks to you as a visual artist, and you'll break new and exciting ground in the crowded field of landscape photography.

Views and Perspective: If you're shooting with a wide-angle lens (24mm and 28mm), as many landscape photographers do, think in terms of threes. Divide the viewfinder horizontally into foreground, middle ground, and background. Now frame, for example, Delicate Arch dead center, and then see how it looks in the foreground, middle ground, and background. What looks best? Let's say the foreground looks good, but you can't fit the snowcapped blue peaks of the La Sal Mountains into the picture. Divide the viewfinder vertically into threes: left, center, and right. Trying framing Delicate Arch in the left foreground; depending on where you've set up your tripod, Delicate Arch and the La Sal Mountains should be framed together. If you want a tighter shot of Delicate Arch framing, say, that twilight moonrise or a La Sal sunset, try using a medium focal length lens (55mm or 85mm), and frame Delicate Arch off center to the right or left of the imaginary line that splits the viewfinder in half. Fill the frame, and work the angles.

Shapes, Colors, Light, Texture, and Water: In terms of shapes, color, light, texture, and water, Canyon Country stands apart. Photographed alone as details or together in a grand panoramic mosaic, these elements make up the breathtaking scenery. Many of these elements are quite obvious; others are more subtle and require keen observation.

Shapes. Volcanic peaks, laccoliths, and craters; mesas, rimrock, cliffs, terraces, and monuments; stair-step, v-shaped, and slot canyons; hoodoos, goblins, balanced rocks, breaks, and badlands; arches, natural bridges, and windows; alcoves, hollows, and caves; and lava flows, boulders, cobbles, pebbles, and sand.

Colors. The wide spectrum of Canyon Country colors can be easily seen in what's called the Grand Staircase in Utah's western Kane County: Chocolate Cliffs, Vermilion Cliffs, White Cliffs, Gray Cliffs, and Pink Cliffs; plus a palette of other colors and shades including red, green, blue, tan, yellow, gold, orange, gray, and black.

Light. Dawn and sunrise; midday shafts of canyon light, refracted light, storm light, lightning, and rainbows; sil-ver river light and mirrored still-water light; and golden hour, sunset, twilight, moonlight, and starlight.

Textures. Slickrock, fossilized sand, desert varnish, orthogonal designs, solution pockets, Moqui balls, cryptobiotic soil, mud, fossils, dinosaur tracks, pictographs, and petroglyphs.

Water. Still water, dew, potholes, and water pockets; moving water, seeps, rain, flash floods, cascades, and waterfalls; and river water, slick water, eddies, whitewater, and foam.

Itinerary: Let's assume time and money are important to you, and you want to photograph Arches National Park. You need to prioritize which icons or vistas you want to shoot and establish a budget and itinerary. What's your out-the-door-ready traveling time from your hotel to the visitor center? Driving or shuttle time from your room or campsite to the vista or trailhead? And hiking time to the vista? Map out your itinerary, what you want to photograph, where each scene is located, and when they're lit with optimal light.

Location Scouting: Scenic drives offer primary access for visitors to many of the viewpoints and popular points of interest to the parks and monuments featured in this book. If you plan to photograph from these scenic drives, take time to scout its viewpoints, and carefully note the best shooting locations for early-morning and late-afternoon light. Many scenic vistas are expensive and/or difficult to reach. So try to precompose two or more distinct images at each location, whether it's two wide-angle landscape images or, say, a wide-angle landscape view, a middle-distance view, and a detail.

Equipment: This is largely a personal choice, what you're comfortable with, what works best for the job, and, if you're a professional, what your clients demand. My gear, like my two-wheel-drive pickup truck, is basic, resilient, and gets the job done in the worst possible environmental conditions: fixed focal length lenses of the highest quality Nikon glass (24mm to 180mm ED); two manual, motor-driven Nikon camera bodies (two camera bodies as backup); Gitzo tripods for stabilizing the camera for long exposures; and a small selection of filters: polarizer, UV haze filter, and graduated neutral-density filter (for exposing for shadow and light). I use Fuji ISO 50 Velvia and 100 Provia, which I keep cooled in blistering summer heat Ziplock bagged in an iced film chest. *Not* the food chest!

Film vs. Digital: Digital is the rage, and if that's your choice of gear, great. For landscape work the vast majority of my clients still demand the highest quality original transparencies for scanning, color separations, and printing. (I don't manipulate my images with Adobe Photoshop, InDesign, Illustrator, or Acrobat Professional.) However, if I were working in one of the globe's hotspots, shooting spot news for a daily newspaper or breaking news for a news weekly, or working as a stalkarazzi (which I couldn't imagine doing even during the leanest times of my career), I would shoot digital exclusively so the time-sensitive images could be transmitted immediately. For assignments on the U.S./Mexico border, I do carry and use a small 5.0 megapixel C-5050 Zoom Olympus digital camera. It has a 3x optical zoom lens (35mm to 105mm), uses xD-Picture Cards, 256MB and 512MB Lexar flashcards, and four rechargeable AA Camedia batteries.

The beauty of using a digital camera on a photo essay is that you can see what you've shot while you're still in the field, and what shots you might be missing to complete the assignment. The flashcards store up to several hundred images, and the camera can shoot a short blast of video if you've encountered a breaking news situation. This camera also works well as a digital "Polaroid" for landscape photography to see what you've shot while you're still on location.

How to Use This Guide

Each of the 38 chapters in this book include "The Story Behind the Scenery" or "The Vista," which include broad strokes and details of each area and what you're seeing; "First Photographed" (who took the first known or published photographs), "Photography" (includes tips but not how I think you should photograph an area—that has to come from you), "Directions," "The Hikes," "Contacts," "Fees," "Backcountry Permits," "Maps," "Neighboring Camera Stops," "Natural Hazards," "Season," and "Natural History Associations." In the back of the book you'll find "Suggested Reading" and the "Trip & Expedition Planner."

Square Tower House, Mesa Verde National Park

I. Mesa Verde National Park

The Vista: Perched on the west slope of the San Juan Mountains between the Colorado and San Juan Rivers, Mesa Verde ("green tablelands") was home to an advanced civilization of ancient cliff dwellers that flourished between A.D. 550 and 1250. Crowned by verdant, subalpine forests, 8,040-foot Mesa Verde is cut by deep slickrock canyons that drain into the Río Mancos, a tributary of the San Juan River. Ancient Pueblo peoples popularly known as the *Anaasází* ("enemy ancestors") built a city of cliff dwellings nestled beneath the rimrock of Mesa Verde's hidden canyons that sheltered them from bitter Rocky Mountain winters and harsh, high-desert summers. Sustained by a vibrant culture, deep spiritual beliefs, and harvests of corn, beans, and squash supplanted with venison and turkey, these indigenous architects and master masons built magnificent multistory dwellings found nowhere else in the United States.

Isolated in the remote, southwestern corner of Colorado off the beaten path of the Old Spanish Trail, Mesa Verde was known only to the Ute, Navajo, and Pueblo peoples who inhabited the area after it was abandoned by the Anaasází. In 1874, however, geologist Ferdinand V. Hayden surveyed Colorado and its neighboring territories for the United States Geological and Geographical Survey, climbing many 14,000-foot peaks to use as triangulation points. Attached to the expedition was veteran Civil War artist-turned-photographer William Henry Jackson. From base camp in Baker's Park, Jackson and naturalist Ernest Ingersoll

Directions: From Cortez, Colorado, drive 10.7 miles east on US 160 to the park turnoff and then 15 miles south to the Far View Visitor Center. From the visitor center, drive 6.5 miles south to the junction of the Cliff Palace and Square Tower House 6-mile loop roads.

The Hikes: Square Tower House, curbside stroll; Cliff Palace, ranger-guided $1/2$-mile round-trip, (500-foot climb); Spruce Tree House, $1/2$-mile round-trip (200-foot climb); and Balcony House, ranger-guided $1/2$-mile round-trip (400-foot climb)

Natural Hazards: On the rim, lightning and exposure; on the trail, steep descents and ascents

Contact: Phone 970-529-4465, or visit www.nps.gov/meve

Entrance Fee: $10 per vehicle for seven days or National Parks Pass

Campground Fee: Morefield Campground, $19 per night, plus tax. Phone 800-449-2288.

Hiking Permits and Fees: Ranger-guided walks $2.75 per person

Maps (optional): USGS 7.5-minute maps: Moccasin Mesa, and Wetherhill Mesa, Colorado

Neighboring Camera Stops: Hovenweep National Monument, Utah

Season: Mid-April to mid-October

Mesa Verde Museum Association: Phone 800-305-6053, or visit www.mesaverde.org

led a pack string of mules into the unexplored Río Mancos region to photograph cliff dwellings that resembled "swallows' nests." Covering 350 miles in two weeks, Jackson produced 40 black-and-white negatives during the journey, including stereoscopic views and 5x8 glass plates. His first stop was Mesa Verde.

"Just as the sun was sinking behind the western walls of the cañon," Jackson wrote on September 9, "one of the party decried far up the cliff what appeared to be a house, with a square wall." Jackson failed to reach the dwelling in the dark, but he returned early the next morning, and the adventure to take the first photographs of Mesa Verde began: "Mexico, our little pack mule, with the apparatus [camera equipment] upon her back, by . . . lively scrambling over the rocks, was able to reach the foot of the precipice," Jackson wrote. "Up this we hauled the boxes containing the camera and chemicals by the long ropes taken from the pack-saddle. One man was shoved up ahead, over the worst place, with the rope, and tying it to a tree, the others easily ascended." Climbing a log wedged against the sheer cliff, Jackson reached hand-carved Anaasází toeholds that lead across the blank face to the two-story cliff dwelling. Perched above a dizzying 800-foot drop, Jackson took "careful views" with his cumbersome 5x8 wooden camera, before lowering it and the fragile glass wet plates over the ledge to the pack string below. The view inspired Jackson to write: "It was worth everything I possessed to stand there and to know, that with Ernest Ingersoll, I was surely the first white man who had ever looked down into the canyon from the dwelling in the cliff."

Ute and Navajo who knew of other storied cliff dwellings avoided the area out of respect for their ancestors. They considered it sacred. But rumors and speculation fueled cowboy-explorer John Wetherhill's quest to find the mysterious cliff dwellings. Wetherhill began searching Mesa Verde's sinuous canyons during the 1880s, but it wasn't until December 18, 1888, that he and Charlie Mason saw Cliff Palace while trailing maverick cattle in a snowstorm. The resulting photographs, publicity, controversial trade in artifacts, and archaeological excavations (which the Ute and Navajo considered pillaging) drew wide attention to Cliff Palace, and led to President Theodore Roosevelt establishing Mesa Verde National Park on June 29, 1906.

Mesa Verde National Park now lures visitors from all over the world to visit extraordinary cliff dwellings that still stand long after contemporary designs have turned to rubble. Once home to 250 to 350 Anaasází, Cliff Palace, Square Tower House, Balcony House, and Spruce Tree House remain the park's showpieces. Viewed from the rim in the copper hue of sunset or the mauve glow of twilight, Square Tower House and Cliff Palace are exquisite edifices designed by indigenous peoples who adapted their architecture to nature's forms.

First Photographed: William Henry Jackson on September 9, 1874. Jackson's photograph of Two Story House is reproduced in his 1940 autobiography, *Time Exposure.* A year after photographing Mesa Verde in 1875, Jackson returned to the Four Corners area to photograph the region's ancient dwellings with a huge 20x24 wet-plate camera! Using a revolu-

Hovenweep Castle, Hovenweep National Monument

tionary Swiss development process called Photochrom ("continuous-tone, full-color reproductions of black-and-white photographs"), Jackson later produced the first color photographs of the Old West. Images from this collection are reproduced in Jim Hughes's 1994 book, *Birth of a Century: Early Color Photographs of America.*

Photography: Scout the vistas early, and you can photograph Square Tower House from the rim in late-afternoon light and Cliff Palace shortly after. In spite of its national park status, Mesa Verde remains sacred to many Native Americans. In deference to their beliefs, I've limited my own views to the rim. Tread gently if you visit these fragile cliff dwellings up close.

Hovenweep National Monument (1)

The Vista: Lost among the canyons, mesas and high deserts between the San Juan River and the rain shadow of the Abajo and La Sal Mountains is a barren tract of empty ground the Ute called *Hovenweep* ("deserted valley"). It was not always so. Inhabited by pre-Columbian peoples for nearly 2,000 years, the Anaasází built masonry dwellings along the rims of the Sage Plain about A.D. 900. Theirs was a hardscrabble existence, hunting, gathering, and tilling terraced plots of corn, beans, and squash before a mega-drought—or possibly marauding enemies—drove them from the region around A.D. 1300. For nearly 400 years, their mesa-top dwellings served as shelters, lookouts, and observation posts. Their square and circular "castle towers" were unique not only for their architectural designs and defense positions, but also because the windows offered commanding vantages of intruders and were aligned for lunar calendars and celestial observations. No one noticed until Mormon pioneer W. D. Huntington reported seeing Hovenweep while leading an expedition through southeast Utah in 1854. Two decades later William Henry Jackson and Ernest Ingersoll led their pack string west from Mesa Verde into the Utah desert to investigate. To the surprise of their lo-

cal guide, Captain John Moss, they discovered Aztec Springs was dry when they reached it the first day beyond the Río Mancos. Nonetheless, Jackson stopped to photograph nearby dwellings and wrote: "It was sunset by the time we had secured the photographic views necessary." They camped in a dry gulch but luckily found a few pools of water to sustain them.

The next morning, Jackson's party traced the dusty course of McElmo Canyon around the flanks of the Sierra El Late (Sleeping Ute Mountain) from one cluster of ruins to the next. At a point on their map called Burial Site, they turned north and reached the trail to Hovenweep. "While passing a wide side-cañon coming in from the right, a tall black-looking tower caught our eye, perched on the very brink of the *mesa,* overlooking the valley," Jackson wrote. "Tying our riding-animals at the foot, and leading the pack-mule, with photographic kit, we soon struck into an old trail, worn deep into the rocks." Jackson guided his mule up the rimrock. Named Hypo, (for the darkroom chemical hyposulfate of soda), the animal was laden with glass plates, a 5x8 wooden camera box, and what Jackson called his "one-mule darkroom." Set against the lofty backdrop of 9,244-foot Sleeping Ute Mountain, the mysterious desert castles stood before them, and on September 13, 1874, Jackson took the first-known

Directions: From Cortez, Colorado, drive 2.7 miles south on US 666. Turn right, and drive 30 miles west on County Road G (McElmo Canyon Road) across the Utah border. Follow the marked turnoffs and drive 10 miles north to the entrance station.

The Hikes: Short walks along the rimrock: $\frac{1}{3}$-mile Square Tower Loop; $\frac{1}{2}$-mile Tower Point Loop; and 1-mile Twin Towers Loop

Contact: Phone 970-562-4282, or visit www.nps.gov/hove

Entrance Fee: $6 per vehicle for seven days or a National Parks Pass

Campgound Fee: $10 per night

Map (optional): USGS 7.5-minute map: Negro Canyon, Colorado (a USGS name)

Neighboring Camera Stops: Mesa Verde National Park, Colorado

Season: All year

Canyonlands Natural History Association: Phone 800-840-8978, or visit www.cnha.org

photographs of Hovenweep. In a dispatch written for the November 3 *New York Tribune,* Ingersoll described the dwellings, the peaceful "sun worshipers" who inhabited them and what he believed led to their demise: "Here they ... erected stone fortifications and watch-towers, dug reservoirs in the rocks to hold a supply of water. . . . Their foes came, and for one long month they fought. . . . [T]he hollows of the rocks were filled to the brim with the mingled blood of conquerors and conquered, and red veins of it ran down into the cañon."

Jackson's photographs and Ingersoll's reporting of ancient watchtowers set against the mythical landscape of the Wild West put Hovenweep on the map. In 1917 the Smithsonian Institution sent J. W. Fewkes to conduct an archaeological survey. Fewkes's enthusiasm led to President Warren G. Harding establishing Hovenweep National Monument on March 2, 1923.

Hovenweep Castle is perched on a rim of bone-white slickrock, and no other desert dwelling I've seen is as captivating to the eye painted with golden brushstrokes of the setting sun.

First Photographed: William H. Jackson on September 13, 1874.

Photography: Hovenweep Castle is best photographed in late afternoon light.

Frijole Falls, Bandelier National Monument

Bandelier National Monument (2)

The Vista: Located on the east slope of the Continental Divide between the Jemez and Sangre de Cristo Mountains, the Pararito Plateau reaches heights of 10,199 feet atop Cerro Grande and plummets a mile to the banks of the Upper Rio Grande. Drained by Frijoles, Alamo, and Capulin Canyons, their turbulent waters cut through layers of volcanic ash, exposing smooth walls in soft tuff. The area was

Directions: From Santa Fe, New Mexico, drive 16 miles north on US 84/285. Turn west on NM 502, and follow the signed turnoffs 27.5 miles to the entrance station.

The Hikes: Frijoles Pueblo Ruins, 2-mile round-trip walk; Upper Frijoles Falls, 2⁶/₁₀-mile round-trip hike (250-foot climb); Lower Frijoles Falls, 3-mile round-trip hike (400-foot climb); and backcountry hikes, varying in length from 12 miles round-trip and longer

Natural Hazards: Lightning during summer monsoons

Contact: Phone 505-672-3861, or visit www.nps.gov/band

Entrance Fee: $10 per vehicle for seven days or a National Parks Pass

Campground Fee: Juniper Campground, $10 per night

Backcountry Permits Required: No charge, phone 505-672-3861, ext. 517

Map (optional): USGS 7.5-minute map: Frijoles, New Mexico

Neighboring Camera Stops: Mesa Verde National Park, Colorado

Season: Mid-April to mid-October

Western National Parks Association: Visit www.wnpa.org

first inhabited by Archaic hunters and gatherers around 1750 B.C., then ancestral Pueblo peoples from A.D. 600 to 1600. Like the Mesa Verde and Hovenweep Anaásazí, they adapted their lifeways and architectural style to nature. Explore the canyons of the *Pajarito* ("little bird") Plateau today, and you will marvel at hand-carved prehistoric cave dwellings, cliff dwellings, and kivas (ceremonial chambers) found nowhere else in the West.

When William H. Jackson photographed Mesa Verde and Hovenweep, he and Ernest Ingersoll had visited what some viewed as Native American "ghost towns," abandoned by a mysterious people called the Anaasází, whose thoughts and beliefs had vanished with them. In contrast, the Pajarito Plateau Adolf F. Bandelier came to know during the 1880s was the ancestral land of modern Pueblo peoples. Their ancient village in Frijoles Canyon was still known by them as *Tyuonyi*. Variously translated in the Keres language to mean "meeting place," it formed an integral part of their oral traditions and spiritual beliefs.

Lured to the Upper Rio Grande by a yearning to discover links between Mesoamerican Indians of Mexico with Pueblo peoples of New Mexico, Bandelier spent eight years in the region, studying the archaeology of the Pajarito Plateau and the ethnology of the Cochití Pueblo people he sometimes lived with. In his 1890 novel, *The Delight Makers*, Bandelier described the refuge Tyuonyi's caves offered its people: "Faster and faster Shotaye ran. . . . [L]ightning tore the clouds, thunder bellowed nearer. . . . Blinded by the torrents of falling water, she groped her way along the walls and finally stumbled into the open door of Say Koitza's home."

Bandelier was not alone in his quest to explore the Pueblo people's ancestral canyon homes. Former *Los Angeles Times* editor Charles F. Lummis was huddling out of the wind in his camp at nearby Los Alamitos one day when Bandelier walked in out of a sandstorm during a 60-mile trek from Zuñi. The pair became lifelong friends, and they explored the New Mexico frontier together: "Thousands of miles of wilderness and desert travel we trudged side by side—camped, starved, shivered, learned," Lummis wrote. "We always went by foot; my big camera and glass plates in the knapsack on my back, the heavy tripod under my arm; [Bandelier carrying] his aneroid, surveying instrument, and satchel of almost microscopic notes. . . . Up and down pathless cliffs, through tangled cañons, fording icy streams and ankle-deep sands, we travailed."

Bandelier's survey and Lummis's photographs put Pajarito Plateau on the map. Edgar Lee Hewett, an archaeologist who surveyed the area from 1908 to 1911, proposed it as a national park. But locals and land claims stalled the matter until President Woodrow Wilson established Bandelier National Monument on February 11, 1916.

Standing at the foot of Long House Ruins today, many visitors can only imagine what it was like to live in a cave. A passage from *The Delight Makers* is reminiscent of Tarahumara homes I've visited in Mexico's Sierra Madre, and I wonder if that was the cultural link Bandelier had sought: "In the fireplace wood was smoldering. . . . In the corner stood the frame for the grinding-slabs, or *metates*. . . . Deerskins and cotton wraps were rolled into a bundle in another corner. . . . After a while a woman's head peeps through the passage. . . . She rises . . . and the sunbeam strikes her features full."

First Photographed: In his 1893 book *The Land of Poco Tiempo* ("little time"), Charles Lummis's photographs illustrate what became Bandelier National Monument. But a photograph taken by George C. Bennett on December 5, 1880—from the Collections of the Museum of New Mexico—depicts Adolf Bandelier with Cochití Pueblo elder Adelaido Montoya standing in front of a Frijoles Canyon cliff dwelling.

Photography: You can photograph Upper and Lower Frijoles Falls in the morning and the Frijoles Pueblo Ruins in the late afternoon.

The Window, Lower Antelope Canyon, Glen Canyon National Recreation Area

II. Glen Canyon National Recreation Area

The Story Behind the Scenery: Draining an estimated 244,000 square miles of the Rocky Mountains and Colorado Plateau, the Colorado River descends more than 10,000 vertical feet from the Continental Divide to the Gulf of California. En route to tidewater 1,400 miles downstream, the Colorado River and its principal tributary, the Green River, have carved a series of tremendous canyons, including Westwater Canyon, Labyrinth and Stillwater Canyons, Cataract Canyon, Glen Canyon, and the Grand Canyon. Of these, none was thought to be more tranquil and beautiful by early explorers than Glen Canyon. When Major John Wesley Powell named it Glen Canyon during his maiden voyage down the Colorado River on August 3, 1869, he wrote: "Past these towering monuments, past these mounded billows of orange sandstone, past these oak-set glens, past these fern-decked alcoves, past these mural curves, we glide hour after hour, stopping now and then, as our attention is arrested by some new wonder."

Stretching 186 miles from Dark Canyon in the northeast to Wahweap Creek in the southwest, Glen Canyon is fed by more than one hundred named canyons, creeks, and gulches, including the San Juan River, Cha Canyon, Forbidden Canyon, Escalante River, and others that bear the names of prospectors, explorers, and Native peoples. Many of these tributaries—beautiful beyond Powell's own descriptions—are deep, narrow gorges that have been cut through Navajo sandstone by eons of flash floods,

Directions: From Page, Arizona, drive 2.5 miles north on US 89 to the Carl Hayden Visitor Center and Glen Canyon Dam

Contact: Phone 928-608-6404, or visit www.nps.gov/glca, www.pagelake powellchamber.org

Entrance Fee: $10 per vehicle for seven days or a National Parks Pass

Boating Fee: $10 per boat for seven days

Camping: Lees Ferry, $10 per night

Primitive Camping: $6 per night

Developed Camping: Phone ARAMARK at 800-528-6154 for fees and locations

Map (optional): USGS 1 x 2 Degree Series, 1:250,000 scale map: Escalante, Utah

Emergencies: Phone 911 or 800-582-4351, or use Marine Band CH-16

Glen Canyon Natural History Association: Phone 928-608-6358, or visit www .glencanyonassociation.org

Glen Canyon Institute: Phone 520-556-9311, or visit www.glencanyon.org

wind, and erosion. Powell and his men often ventured into these mysterious chasms and discovered lost secrets of the Anaasází, who inhabited Glen Canyon from A.D. 750 to 1300.

Crossed in 1776 by Spanish padres Francisco Atanasio Domínguez and Silvestre Vélez de Escalante at *El Vado de los Padres* ("The Crossing of the Fathers") Glen Canyon was later traversed by adventurers who followed Powell's lead, including photographers and explorers Emery and Ellsworth Kolb. Between 1911 and1913 the Kolb brothers ran the

Green and Colorado Rivers from Green River, Wyoming, to the Gulf of California. While rowing the Colorado River above the San Juan River, Ellsworth described the mystical light: "We again entered a deep canyon; sheer for several hundred feet, creamy white above. . . . [A] glorious full moon had risen, spreading a soft weird light over the canyon walls and the river."

The small cadre of modern boatmen, canyoneers, and photographers who later explored Glen Canyon considered it paradise on earth until construction of Glen Canyon Dam was completed in 1964. When the wild waters of the Colorado River filled Lake Powell to full capacity at 3,700 feet during the winter of 1980–81, its epitaph was written: "The Place No One Knew." A prolonged drought has dropped water levels to 3,550 feet, and flooded canyons have emerged from the brine. Environmentalists are proposing Glen Canyon Dam be decommissioned in hopes of restoring Glen Canyon to a near-natural state that Native Americans, explorers, and a handful of photographers were once privy to witness.

First Photographed: E. O. Beaman, James Fennemore and John K. "Jack" Hillers first photographed Glen Canyon during Powell's second Colorado River Expedition in 1871–72. Their pioneer photographs illustrate Powell's 1875 account of his explorations, and expedition artist Frederick S. Dellenbaugh's two classic books: *Romance of the Colorado River* (1902), and *A Canyon Voyage* (1908). Before Glen Canyon was lost, two modern photographers also captured its extraordinary beauty. Eliot Porter's lush color photographs were first and illustrate

his 1963 book, *The Place No One Knew: Glen Canyon on the Colorado.* Tad Nichol's elegant black-and-white images were last and adorn his 1999 book *Glen Canyon: Images of the Lost World.*

Photography: Each year tens of thousands of visitors venture into Glen Canyon's slickrock canyons and camp along

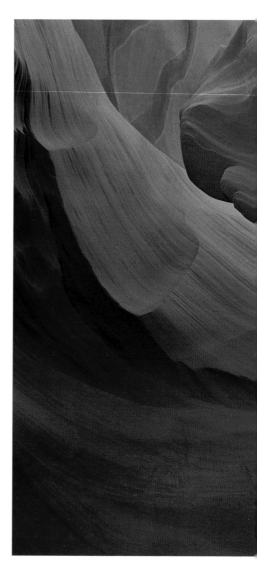

its 1,900 miles of shoreline. Most do so by houseboat or speedboat. But a growing number of adventurers and photographers are exploring its wonderful side canyons in canoes and sea kayaks from below and by foot from above. You can spend a week, a season, or a lifetime photographing Glen Canyon's hidden corridors, secret alcoves, and natural wonders.

Lower Antelope Canyon (3)

The Vista: Few of Glen Canyon's sublime tributary canyons are more beautiful—or have proven more deadly—than Lower Antelope Canyon. Earth crack, incised meander, narrows, corridor of stone, slot canyon—simple descriptions fail to describe a cathedral of stone illumi-

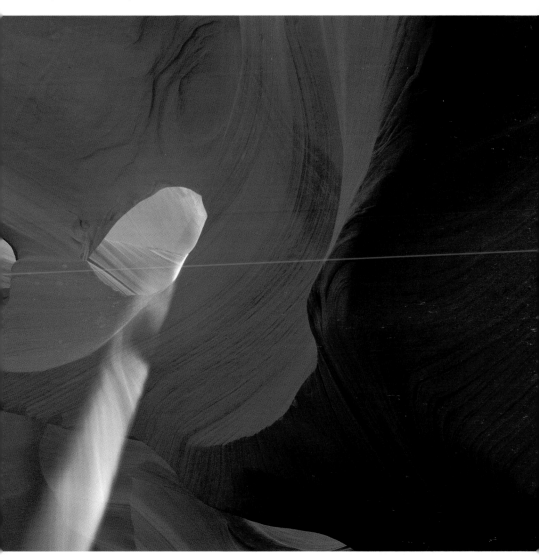

The Eye, Lower Antelope Canyon, Glen Canyon National Recreation Area

Directions: From US 89 south of Page, Arizona, drive 5 miles east on AZ 98 to the Antelope Point Road (N 22). Turn north, and drive a short distance to the Lower Antelope Canyon turnoff.

The Hike: A short, enjoyable scramble. Rancher and photographer Ken Young has installed safety ladders for access and rigged nylon ladders that can be used for escape.

Natural Hazards: Claustrophobia and deadly flash floods. Though warned of the impending danger, 12 tourists lost their lives in a flash flood that swept down Lower Antelope Canyon on August 1, 1997. Navajo Nation Parks closes the entrance during flash flood danger.

Contact: Phone Ken Young's Tours 928-660-2844, or email keny@aztrail.com

Entrance Fee: Navajo Nation Parks, $6 per person

Day Use Fee: $12.50 per adult, $10 per child (7–12 years old)

Map (optional): USGS 7.5-minute map: Page, Arizona

Neighboring Camera Stops: Upper Antelope Canyon, Horseshoe Bend, Coyote Buttes, Buckskin Gulch, Paria Canyon, Lees Ferry, Balanced Rocks, Echo Cliffs, and Vermilion Cliffs National Monument. (See *The Photographer's Guide to the Grand Canyon* by this author; phone Countryman Press at 800-245-4151, or visit www.countrymanpress.com).

Season: Open all year during dry weather. Call ahead to check the local weather and forecast: 928-660-2844.

nated by the golden rays of a yellow sun. Enter the head of this sacred canyon, called *Hasdestwazi*, "spiral rock arches," and you are at once struck by the fossilized waves of copper-colored stone. Follow its narrow, serpentine bed and you will enter a subterranean world of enchantment. Climb down the stairwells, and you descend farther into what feels like the center of the earth. Probe beyond your natural fears, and you will cross over into a realm that time has seemingly forgotten. You have reached the underworld, as cut off from modern civilization as you can be this close to the blacktop. Everywhere you turn sensual forms please your eyes and soothe your soul. Nature will cast her spell. You will be hypnotized by heavenly beams of light. And once you emerge from this dreamscape, you will tell anyone who will listen that it's *in*credible, uhhh-mazing, un-BE-liev-able. They will roll their eyes, "Uh-huh." So don't say a word. Show them the pictures.

First Photographed: James Fennemore and Jack Hillers took the first known photograph of a Glen Canyon "side canyon" during Powell's second Colorado River Expedition on July 2, 1872. Fennemore's and Jackson's photograph was reproduced in Dellenbaugh's 1902 book, *Romance of The Colorado River.*

Photography: Midmorning and late afternoon. Take your time. Follow the light. Here, as elsewhere, seek your own vision. Lower Antelope Canyon is a welcome contrast to the throngs of visitors who stampede through nearby Upper Antelope Canyon.

Rainbow Bridge National Monument (4)

The Vista: Few natural wonders in the West inspired explorers more than Rainbow Bridge. Steeped in the legends of prospectors, mysterious sightings by Paiute guides, and the holy beliefs of Navajo medicine men, Rainbow Bridge was a coveted prize for non-Indians bent on discovering the largest natural bridge in the world. Standing 290 feet tall and spanning 275 feet, Rainbow Bridge lay hidden beneath the rugged flanks of 10,388-foot Navajo Mountain on the Utah-Arizona border. Inhabited by the Anaasází from A.D. 750 to 1300, the remote Canyon Country encircling Rainbow Bridge became the domain of the Paiute, Ute, and Navajo. Fleeing the scorched-earth campaign of Christopher "Kit" Carson in 1863, many Navajo sought refuge behind Navajo Mountain. They called it *Naatsis'áán,* "head of the Earth." It was the Divine Shield that protected them.

First seen by Navajo medicine man Blind Salt Clansman in 1868, Rainbow Bridge became known as *Na'nízhoozhí,* "rainbow rock-span," and it figured prominently in Navajo Mountain and Rainbow Bridge religion. Located near the confluence of the Colorado River and San Juan River, the Cloud and Rain People were born from their sacred waters and were joined together at Rainbow Bridge. Since the 1870s Navajo medicine men have made pilgrimages to Rainbow Bridge to perform the sacred Protectionway and Blessingway healing ceremonies But it soon became apparent to outsiders that Rainbow Bridge's deep religious significance dated at least as far back as the Anaasází. When Teddy Roosevelt visited Rainbow Bridge on August 13, 1913, he wrote: "The arch is the sign of the rainbow, the sign of the sun's course over the earth, and to the Navajo it is sacred. This great natural bridge, so recently "discovered" by white men, has for ages been known to the Indians.... [A]lmost under it there is what appears to be the ruin of a very ancient shrine."

It was into this hallowed country that John Wetherhill headed up the joint Douglass-Cummings Expedition to "discover" Rainbow Bridge during August 1909. Led on horseback across the slickrock by Paiute guides Jim Mike and Nasja Begay, government surveyor W. B. Douglass and archaeologist Dean Byron Cummings claimed discovery of Rainbow Bridge on August 14. In a statement made by W. F. Williams on May 22, 1929, however, the prospector said that Hosteen Hoskininni, a great Navajo chief and medicine man, led him and his father, J. Patterson Williams, to Rainbow Bridge during the winter of 1884. Williams's party might have claimed discovery of Rainbow Bridge, but he said: "There were names cut on the base of . . . Rainbow Bridge when we saw it." The names included Billy Ross, Jim Black, George Emmerson, Ed Randolph, and two men named Wydell and Montgomery. Photographs taken by photographer Stuart M. Young during the Douglass-Cummings Expedition would have undoubtedly trumped Williams's statement if he'd intended to refute their claim.

Inspired by the Douglass-Cummings visit, President William Howard Taft established Rainbow Bridge National Monument on May 30, 1910, and the rush to be the next expedition to make the rugged overland trek to the great bridge was on. Appointed caretaker of the monument for $1 a month, Wetherhill's client list included Teddy Roosevelt, Zane Grey, Emery and Ellsworth Kolb, and others. But it was Grey who summed up the journey best when he wrote: "Rainbow

---

Directions: From Page, Arizona, drive 43 miles southeast on AZ 98 to the Inscription House turnoff. Drive north 13.5 miles on N16 until the pavement turns to dirt. Turn left (north), and drive 18.6 miles to the Navajo Mountain junction. Turn left (northwest), and drive 5.8 miles to the historic Rainbow Lodge site.

The Trek: From the Rainbow Lodge site at 6,400 feet, the undeveloped Rainbow Bridge Trail is 13 miles one way, (elevation loss: 2,500 vertical feet). This was the route of the 1922 Wetherhill-Bernheimer Expedition. Cache food and water on the descent and return the same way. Or follow the undeveloped 12½- mile long Navajo Mountain Trading Post Trail around the north side of Navajo Mountain to a shuttle vehicle at Cha Canyon trailhead. This was the route of 1909 Wetherhill Douglass-Cummings Expedition. I followed the Rainbow Bridge Trail to Rainbow Bridge, returned via Navajo Mountain Trading Post Trail to Owl Bridge, scrambled up the summit of Navajo Mountain, and hiked down the high-clearance dirt road past War God Spring to Navajo Mountain Trading Post.

Mileposts and Elevations (±):

Mile 1: First Canyon (6,200 feet)

Mile 2: Horse Canyon (6,200 feet)

Mile 5: Yabut Pass (6,400 feet), 1,600-foot descent to Cliff Canyon

Mile 7: Cliff Canyon (4,800 feet), follow streambed

Mile 8: First Water campsite

Mile 9: Redbud Pass junction, turn right (northeast)

Mile 9.4: Redbud Pass, 1922 Wetherhill-Bernheimer inscription

Mile 10: Redbud Creek, follow streambed north-northwest

Mile 10.6: Prehistoric dwellings

Mile 10.9: Bridge Creek and Navajo Mountain Trading Post Trail junction; turn left (west), and follow Bridge Creek downstream

Mile 12: Bridge Creek milepost

Mile 12.7: Drift fence and gate; close gate

Mile 12.8: Echo Spring and campsite

Mile 13: Rainbow Bridge (3,900 feet). In deference to Navajo spiritual beliefs, don't walk under or climb to the top of Rainbow Bridge.

Natural Hazards: Lightning, flash floods, rock fall, and rugged terrain

Contact: Rainbow Bridge National Monument, phone 520-608-6404, or visit www.nps.gov/rabr

Backcountry Permits and Fees: Navajo Nation Parks, phone 928-871-6636, or visit www.navajonationparks.org and www.discovernavajo.com

Maps (required): USGS 7.5-minute maps: Chaiyahi Flat, Arizona, and Rainbow Bridge, Utah–Arizona

Neighboring Camera Stops: Upper Antelope Canyon, Arizona

Season: Spring through fall

Canyonlands Field Institute: Periodically offers pack stock–supported treks to Rainbow Bridge. Phone 800-860-5262, or visit www.canyonlandsfieldinst.org.

Bridge was not for many eyes to see. The tourist, the leisurely traveler, the comfort loving . . . would never behold it. Only by toil, sweat, endurance, and pain could any man ever look at *nonnezoshe* [sic]. It seemed well to realize that the great things in life had to be earned." I agree.

First Photographed: Navajo Mountain was first photographed by John K. Hillers from the Kaiparowits Plateau on June 6, 1872, while searching for the Dirty Devil River with Powell's overland expedition. Hillers's photograph is reproduced in Dellenbaugh's 1908 book, *A Canyon Voyage.* But Rainbow Bridge wasn't photographed until August 14, 1909, when Douglass-Cummings Expedition photographer Stuart M. Young took the first set of photographs. Young's photographs are reproduced in Hank Hassell's 1999 book, *Rainbow Bridge: An Illustrated History.*

During their journey down the Colorado River in 1911, Emery and Ellsworth Kolb planned to take the first motion pictures of Rainbow Bridge, but their directions to reach it from the river were vague, and they unknowingly drifted past the mouth of Forbidden Canyon. The Kolbs returned with John Wetherill and photographed Rainbow Bridge in September 1913. The Kolbses' photograph was reproduced in Ellsworth's 1914 book, *Through the Grand Canyon from Wyoming to Mexico.*

Photography: You can follow the wakes of tens of thousands of visitors who travel by speedboat and houseboat to the foot of Rainbow Bridge each year. Or you can follow the trail of medicine men, explorers, writers, and pioneer photographers across the sacred landscape to the foot of the rainbow.

Portrait, Rainbow Bridge National Monument

III. Grand Staircase–Escalante National Monument

The Story Behind the Scenery: A stark, beautiful no-man's-land the size of Washington, D.C., Rhode Island, and Delaware, Grand Staircase–Escalante National Monument remains frozen in time. Rugged, remote, and undeveloped, its desolate beauty ranges from the seldom-explored slickrock canyons of the Escalante River to the caprock hoodoos of Jack Riggs Bench and the stone goblins of Devils Garden. Few parks in the West are as wild and enticing for photographers in

Wahweap Creek, Grand Staircase–Escalante National Monument

search of new horizons than southern Utah's Grand Staircase–Escalante National Monument.

Established by President Bill Clinton in 1996 under the century-old Antiquities Act, the 1.7-million-acre monument was the homeland of the Southern Paiute. Since the days of the ancestral Mukwic ("People We Never Saw"), the Kaibab and Kaiparowits bands of Paiute adapted their

lifeways and culture to the area's austere geography. Divided into three sections, the western third of Grand Staircase–Escalante National Monument is called Grand Staircase. Its multihued terraces stair step up from the high desert of the Chocolate Cliffs, Vermilion Cliffs, White Cliffs, and Gray Cliffs to the Pink Cliffs of the forested Paunsaugunt Plateau. The middle third is called the Kaiparowits Plateau, and it is characterized by the arid and lofty 50-mile-long plateau, the 100-mile-long Cockscomb, and the Straight Cliffs. The eastern third is called Escalante Canyons. Carved by the main stem of the Escalante River, it's fed by seasonal rivers rushing through seldom-visited, extraordinarily beautiful slickrock canyons.

Surrounded by daunting, nearly insurmountable barriers such as the Vermilion Cliffs and Glen Canyon on the south, the Cockscomb and Paunsaugunt Plateau on the west, the Aquarius Plateau on the north, and Waterpocket Fold on the east, the Grand Staircase–Escalante National Monument area remained the last unexplored region in the contiguous United States. Avoided by the Domínguez and Escalante Expedition, which nearly looped around the region in 1776, few early travelers had reason to traverse the Southern Paiute's hauntingly beautiful domain.

Among those who did was surveyor Almon Harris Thompson, photographer John K. Hillers, and artist Frederick S. Dellenbaugh. Assigned by Major John Wesley Powell to locate the source of a Colorado River tributary that Powell named the Dirty Devil River, the overland expedition was the first to explore, map, write about, and photograph the uncharted region between May 29 and July

Directions: From Kanab, Utah, drive
1.5 miles east on US 89 to the Kanab
Visitor Center and Grand Staircase–
Escalante National Monument head-
quarters

Contact: Phone 435-644-4680, or visit
www.ut.blm.gov/monument

Maps and Guide, (optional): USGS 1 x 2
Degree Series, 1: 250,000 Scale region
map: Escalante, Utah. The 1997
"Grand Staircase–Escalante National
Monument" map and brochure is the
best complimentary guide published
by a national park or monument.

Glen Canyon Natural History Association:
Phone 877-453-6296, or visit
www.glencanyonassociation.org

7, 1872. They are credited with discovering the Escalante River, "the last major
river discovered in the United States,"
and traversing the Henry Mountains, then
called the Unknown Mountains. When
the party climbed to the top of the Kaiparowits Plateau on June 6, Dellenbaugh
described the discovery of the Escalante
River: "The question was, 'What river is
this?' for we had not noted a tributary of

any size between the Dirty Devil and the
San Juan. It was a new river whose identity
had not been fathomed. This discovery
put a different complexion on everything."

Follow the ancient trails of the Southern Paiute and the routes of Powell's men,
and you will embark on a photographic
adventure few developed national parks
can offer. Travel into the great American
outback of Grand Staircase, and the immense landscape will envelop you. You
are off the grid, and you are on your own.
You will see nature face to face without
blight, crowds, or traffic. Your vision is
unfettered, and few scenic images dictate
how it might be photographed.

First Photographed: John K. Hillers first
photographed the summit of the Kaiparowits Plateau in the foreground of his
photograph of Navajo Mountain on June
6, 1872. Hillers's photograph was reproduced in Dellenbaugh's 1908 book, *A
Canyon Voyage.*

Photography: You can spend a week, a
season, or a lifetime photographing the
primeval wonders of this modern no-
man's-land.

Wahweap Hoodoos (5)

The Vista: Few formations in Grand Staircase–Escalante National Monument are as unworldly and beautiful as its caprock hoodoos. Produced over eons

Directions: From Page, Arizona, drive 16 miles north on US 89 to the Big Water Visitor Center. Drive across US 89 north through Big Water, Utah 3.5 miles past the fish hatchery to Nipple Creek. If dry, cross Nipple Creek and drive another half mile to the confluence of Coyote, Wahweap, and Nipple Creeks, and park along the high-clearance-vehicle dirt road.

The Hike: Follow the main stem of Wahweap Creek cross country 4 miles north to the first white-rock hoodoos on the west. Several unmaintained trails lead through the tamarisk to the base of the hoodoos. **Use Extreme Care!** Do not climb around these fragile monuments. Careless footprints and rogue four-wheel-drive tracks that trace Wahweap Creek through the Wilderness Study Area indicate the hoodoos are in jeopardy. The Bureau of Land Management should protect these remarkable treasures.

Natural Hazards: Flash floods during summer monsoons

Backcountry and Camping Permits: Available free at the Big Water Visitor Center. Phone 435-675-3200, or visit www.ut.blm.gov/monument

Maps (optional): USGS 7.5-minute map: Glen Canyon City, and Nipple Butte, Utah

Neighboring Camera Stops: Lower Antelope Canyon, Arizona

Season: All year during dry weather

Hoodoos, Grand Staircase–Escalante National Monument

when the soft underlying mud and silt stone of the Entrada Sandstone eroded beneath the hard caprock of the Dakota Formation, these fragile yet haunting white shale, black stone figures are not landmarks that most locals—or visitors—associate with the scenic West. Called the "Towers of Silence" by some, you will be awed standing in the presence of these wonderfully strange monuments. The first-known outsider to visit the area was Powell surveyor Almon Harris Thomson. In 1872 Thompson traversed the Paria

River between Bryce Canyon's Pink Cliffs and Glen Canyon's El Vado de Los Padres, "Crossing of the Fathers." Thompson's diary is as lean as horse jerky, but he made several entries indicating that he may have been the first to view Wahweap Creek's "sentinels." Thompson noted: "Wednesday, August 25th. Came to camp about 12 miles above Paria settlement. 25 miles. Thursday, 26th. Came to camp about 9 miles below the old settlement. Camped with Navajos, 18 miles. Friday, August 27th. Came to a camp in Sentinel Rock Wash [Wahweap Creek], about 20 miles." When I first photographed these hoodoos, I felt like I was visiting country few had seen. Reflecting back on my overland journey to Rainbow Bridge, I wondered if the Southern Paiute hadn't made sacred pilgrimages to the area to revere ancestral spirits these hoodoos may have represented. If the original name Sentinel Rock Wash is descriptive, these hoodoos served as wonderful mileposts for other early travelers.

First Photographed: It isn't known who took the first photographs of these hoodoos.

Photography: Morning is the best time to photograph these east-facing hoodoos. To catch first light, you need to walk in the same day at "o'dark-thirty," or backpack in and camp the afternoon prior. In direct sunlight, these hoodoos are as white as snow, so you'll need to overexpose 1 to 1½ stops to get the correct exposure.

Grosvenor Arch (6)

The Vista: Standing over Cottonwood Creek on the western brink of the Cockscomb, this landmark arch is unique for its double span. Driving through the piñon and juniper across the Butler Valley toward the 6,511-foot formation called The Gut, you won't see Grosvenor Arch until the last moment. Named in honor of National Geographic Society president Gilbert Grosvenor, who was also editor of *National Geographic* magazine, the arch appears to be less than 200 feet tall. Were it not for 6,500-foot (±) Grosvenor Arch, it would still be worth the journey across the slickrock benches from Kodachrome Basin to see the area around it.

First Photographed: The first published photographs of Grosvenor Arch may have been taken by Jack Breed in 1947 for his

Directions: From the Cannonville Visitor Center in Cannonville, Utah, drive 7.4 miles south on the paved road to Kodachrome Basin State Park turnoff. Follow the dirt road 10.7 miles east to the Grosvenor Arch parking area.

The Hike: A short walk on a paved trail leads to the foot of the arch

Natural Hazards: Lightning and flash floods during monsoons

Backcountry and Camping Permits: Available free at the Cannonville Visitor Center. Phone 435-826-5640, or visit www.ut.blm.gov/monument.

Maps (optional): USGS 7.5-minute maps: Butler Valley, Slickrock Bench, Henrieville, and Cannonville, Utah

Neighboring Camera Stops: Kodachrome Basin State Park, Utah

Season: All year during dry weather

Grosvenor Arch, Grand Staircase-Escalante National Monument

1949 *National Geographic* story, "First Motor Sortie in Escalante Land."

Photography: Grosvenor Arch is best photographed in early morning and late afternoon. When Jack Breed photographed Grosvenor Arch, he took two published views. He stood at the foot of it and photographed the arch cradling a piñon tree—as most photographers now do. But he also climbed the bluff behind Grosvenor Arch to show a different, rarely seen view.

Metate Arch, Devils Garden, Grand Staircase-Escalante National Monument

Devils Garden (7)

The Vista: Wandering with camera and tripod amongst the stone goblins of Devils Garden is delightful and surprising at nearly every turn. How anyone but a zealot could call such a whimsical and fantastic landscape the garden of the devil is puzzling. Faces and figures resembling character's from *Alice in Wonderland* loom over you in what feels more like a photographer's playground. Perched on the rimrock above Right Hand Collet Canyon, these megalithic Entrada Sandstone pillars have captivated photographers since Powell's men visited the area while searching for the elusive Dirty Devil River. The "Goblins" were named in 1875 by Almon Harris Thompson, who makes it undeniably clear in his diary that Hillers reached—and photographed—this exact location: "Thursday, August 5th. Came from camp on Last Chance [Collet Wash] to a camp on Pine Creek about a mile above its junction with the Escalante. Saw four Mormons from Panguitch who are talking about making a settlement here. Advised them to call the place Escalante. Jack [Hillers] took three views of the 'Goblins.'"

First Photographed: John K. Hillers took the first-known photographs of Devils Garden between August 5 and August 9, 1875. (I have not seen these photographs.) At the time, Hillers also took the first-known photograph of Devils Garden's Metate Arch, then called "the Goblin's Archway." This photograph was reproduced in Don D. Fowler's 1989 book, *Myself in the Water: The Western Photographs of John K. Hillers.* Three years earlier Hillers and James Fennemore also took the first-known photographs of Escalante River Canyon at Harris Wash on June 6, 1872. Hillers diary entry for that day's efforts reads: "Fen[nemore] and myself started down the gulch for some pictures. After going about a mile we came to a jump down of nearly a thousand feet deep, while the walls above us measured nearly the same. . . . [the] top of a Cañon being nearly 2,000 feet wide while at the bottom on[ly] six feet, no water being in it, only in [water] pocket. Photographed it and two other views, and then returned to camp." One of their views, called "Lateral Canyon," was reproduced in Dellenbaugh's 1902 book, *The Romance of The Colorado River*.

Photography: Early morning and late afternoon are the best times to photograph Devils Garden. Mid- to late afternoon is often best to photograph the Escalante Canyons.

Directions: From the Escalante Visitor Center in Escalante, Utah, drive 5.4 miles east on UT 12 to the Hole-in-the-Rock Road turnoff. Drive 12.3 miles south on this graded dirt road to the Devils Garden turnoff and another ¼ mile to the parking and picnic area.

The Hike: A sandy, unmaintained ½-mile-long trail leads through the hoodoos and slickrock

Escalante Canyons: From Utah Highway 12, you can drive south down the 57-mile Hole-in-the-Rock Road and access the following tributary canyons of the Escalante River:

Mileposts (±) and Canyons:

Mile 00.0: Highway 12

Mile 10.8: Harris Wash: Turn left (east) and drive 6.3 miles to trailhead. It's 10.5 miles to Escalante River.

Mile 12.3: Devils Garden: Turn right (west)

Mile 26.6: Dry Fork of Coyote Gulch: Turn left, and drive 1.7 miles to reach these slot canyons:

Dry Fork: Descend 100 yards to streambed; turn left (1–2 miles long)

Peek-a-Boo: From Dry Fork streambed, turn right, walk a quarter mile downstream, and scramble 12 feet up to canyon entrance (quarter mile long)

Spooky: From Peek-a-Boo, walk a half mile downstream to canyon on left (quarter mile)

Mile 34.7: Hurricane Wash: Turn left, and drive to the corral. It's 13.2 miles to the Escalante River.

Mile 37.8: Dance Hall Rock: Roadside stroll

Mile 42.7: Willow Gulch: Turn left, and drive 1.5 miles to end. It's 3 miles to Broken Bow Arch.

Mile 52: Davis Gulch: Pull out and park. It's 5 miles to the vicinity of Everett Ruess's last camp.

Mile 57: Hole-in-the-Rock: Park. It's a steep quarter-mile scramble down this pioneer Mormon wagon route to what once was the Colorado River.

Natural Hazards: Lightning and flash floods during monsoons

Backcountry and Camping Permits: Available free at the Escalante Visitor Center. Phone 435-826-5499, or visit www.ut.blm.gov/monument

Maps (optional): USGS 7.5-minute maps: For Devils Garden, see Seep Flat and Tenmile Flat, Utah

Neighboring Camera Stops: Canyons of the Escalante River and Coyote Gulch. See above.

Season: All year during dry weather

Sand Pipe, Kodachrome Basin State Park

Kodachrome Basin State Park (8)

The Vista: The wonderfully strange red monoliths of this high desert are akin to something you'd expect to see in the Australian outback. Reportedly ranging from 6 to nearly 170 feet tall, 70 recorded sand pipes, spires, chimneys, and turrets loom over a pygmy forest of piñon and juniper. Kodachrome Basin, however, would be dwarfed by the largest monolith in the world, Australia's 1,143-foot-tall Ayers Rock, called *Uluru* by aboriginal people. Together with nearby *Kata Tjuta*, "Place of Many Heads," the sacred stones are at the center of aboriginal legend, their ancient paintings, and their spiritual universe. Sitting next to a campfire in the American outback at the foot of a towering black monument that's backlit by star-streaked heavens, I wonder if the Kaibab Paiute didn't view their towering sandstone pillars and sky-scraping red walls with the same reverence. What the Paiute may have named the formations, what prayers and talismans they may have offered, and whether they represented benevolent or evil spirits is not known, having been lost to oral tradition. Turn-of-the-last-century ethnographers provide few clues as to what may have, indeed,

his 1949 *National Geographic* magazine story, "First Motor Sortie into Escalante Land." Then known as Thorny Pasture, *National Geographic* proposed that the name be changed to Kodachrome Basin. With the blessing of the Kodak Film Company, the name was changed in 1949.

Photography: The area is best photographed in early morning, late afternoon, and twilight.

been a sacred area. It's not difficult to imagine a Kaibab healing ceremony being performed here: yellow flames licking the dark heavens, the sound of beating drums as shadows dance against the walls.

Painted Uluru red in the setting sun, the Entrada Sandstone monuments will captivate your eyes, your imagination, and your camera lens. Today, Kodachrome Basin lures visitors and photographers down the "All-American Highway" into this remote corner of the Utah desert.

First Photographed: The first-published photographs of Kodachrome Basin may have been taken by Jack Breed in 1947 for

Directions: From the Grand Staircase–Escalante National Monument Visitor Center in Cannonville, Utah, drive 7.4 miles south on the paved road to the Kodachrome Basin turnoff, then drive 2.3 miles north to the park entrance and campground

The Hikes: Nature Trail, ½-mile loop (paved); Eagle View Trail, ½-mile round-trip (500-foot climb); Angels Palace Trail, ½-mile loop (100-foot climb); Sentinel Trail, 1-mile round-trip; Grand Parade Trail, 1½-mile loop (equestrian trail); and Panorama Trail, 3-mile loop (equestrian and bicycle trail)

Natural Hazards: Lightning and flash floods during summer monsoons

Contact: Phone 435-679-8562, or visit www.stateparks.utah.gov

Entrance Fee: $5 per night

Campground Fee: $14 per night. Phone 800-322-3770 for reservations.

Day Use: $12 for five days

Maps (optional): USGS 7.5-minute maps: Henrieville and Cannonville, Utah

Neighboring Camera Stops: Grosvenor Arch, Grand Staircase–Escalante National Monument, Utah

Season: All year

IV. Zion National Park

Zion Canyon Scenic Drive

The Story Behind the Scenery: Zion National Park is a classic American landscape. Majestic, bold, and beautiful, no other topography in the West is quite like it. Towering white walls and colossal buttresses may remind you of Yosemite and Sequoia National Parks. Hanging gardens and deep, narrow canyons may remind you of Glen Canyon National Recreation Area. But that's where the comparisons stop. Located on the western rim of the Colorado Plateau, Zion Canyon is

Court of the Patriarchs, Zion National Park

bordered on the north by the Great Basin Desert, on the west by the Mojave Desert, and on the east by the Painted Desert. Ranging from the subalpine forests of the 8,500-foot Kolob Terrace to the riparian Sonoran Desert habitat of the Virgin River at 3,747 feet, Zion Canyon was formed over a period of 240 million years by water, wind, and erosion sculpting the 2,000-foot-thick fossilized dunes of Navajo sandstone. Plentiful game, de-

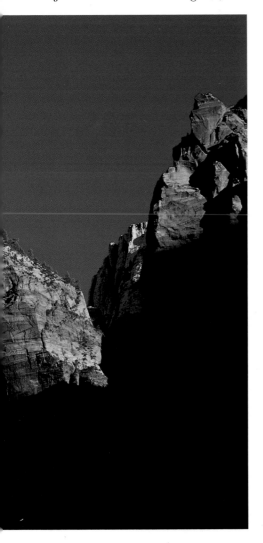

pendable water, fertile soil, and, no doubt, its inspiring setting, lured the Anaasází into the area between A.D. 500 and 1200. The Parrusits band of Southern Paiute later occupied the region, hunting, gathering, and farming, until they were displaced by pioneers and settlers.

Bypassed by mountain man Jedediah Strong Smith while following the Spanish Trail along the lower course of the Virgin River to San Gabriel, California in 1826, Paiute guides led Mormon missionary Nephi Johnson to the mouth of Zion Canyon in September 1858. Johnson traveled alone up the North Fork of the Virgin River and later reported to his brethren that the pastures there were greener still. Named Little Zion Valley by pioneers—or church elder Brigham Young—farmers and cattle and sheep ranchers began settling the area in 1861. Nine years later missionary explorer Jacob Hamblin led Major John Wesley Powell into the region, and they became the first non-Indians to venture through its immense canyons. Descending the East Fork of the Virgin River through Parunuweap Canyon, Powell's party turned north up Zion Canyon and followed the North Fork of the Virgin River into Zion Narrows. On September 12, 1870, Powell wrote: "The [Paiute] Indians call the cañon through which it runs Mu-koon-tu-weap, or Straight Cañon."

Visiting Little Zion Valley on the heels of Powell's expedition, John Hillers took the first-known photographs of Little Zion Valley. Geologist Herbert E. Gregory wrote: "The photographs by J. K. Hillers of the Gate to Zion, the Court of the Patriarchs, and Angels Landing for the first time called attention to features that gave Zion National Park its fame."

The reports of Powell expedition geologist Clarence E. Dutton and boatman Frederick S. Dellenbaugh only added to the region's renown. Dellenbaugh wrote: "The spectator is instantly enveloped in the maze of cliffs and color, a double line of majestic sculptures—domes, pyramids, pinnacles, temples, sweeping away to the north, dazzling with vermillion, orange, pink and white—all scintillating in the burning sunlight with an intensity not comprehensible to those who have never had the good fortune to breathe this lambent air amidst the overwhelming profusion of color." On July 31, 1909, President William Howard Taft established Mukuntuweap National Monument, but locals resisted the Paiute name Powell had used. The name was changed to Zion National Park In 1919.

First Photographed: John K. Hillers and James Fennemore took the first-known photographs of Zion Canyon and Court of the Patriarchs on April 28–29, 1872. These photographs were reproduced in Dellenbaugh's 1902 book, *The Romance of The Colorado River*. Fennemore also photographed Hillers standing on the edge of the rimrock thousands of feet above what was then called Mukuntuweap Valley. Fennemore's image, which rivals the view and exposure at Angels Landing, (see below), was reproduced in Don D. Fowler's 1989 book, *Myself in the Water*. In the early 1900s, park rangers began showing tourists hand-colored lantern slides. Taken by a variety of photographers, these images are reproduced in J. L. Crawford's 1986 book, *Zion Album: A Nostalgic History of Zion Canyon*.

Photography: Many of Zion National Park's most famous landmarks can be photographed from the 7.1-mile Zion Canyon Scenic Drive, which now follows the historic route of Paiutes, explorers, and settlers through Zion Canyon. Scout Zion Canyon Scenic Drive beforehand.

Stops and Viewpoints

Stop 1: Towers of the Virgin. The Towers of the Virgin include (left to right) the 6,364-foot Three Marys, the 7,810-foot West Temple, the 7,438-foot Sun Dial, and the 7,410-foot Altar of Sacrifice. Poet-geologist Clarence E. Dutton described the view in his 1882 *Tertiary History of the Grand Cañon District, With Atlas:* "In an instant there flashed before us a scene never to be forgotten . . . the most exquisite of its kind which [sic] the world discloses. The scene before us was the Temples and Towers of the Virgin." Get up at dawn to photograph the view at first light. *Location:* Behind the Human History Museum.

Stop 2: Court of the Patriarchs. The Court of the Patriarchs includes (left to right) 6,990-foot Abraham, 6,825-foot Isaac, 6,831-foot Jacob, and 5,690-foot Mount Moroni. (It was 16-year-old Claud Hirschi who, while visiting Zion Canyon in 1916, named the Three Patriarchs after Old Testament figures.) You should have plenty of time to photograph the Court of the Patriarchs in the early morning after photographing the Towers of the Virgin. *Location:* Between the Human History Museum and Zion Lodge.

Stop 3: Great White Throne. The 6,744-foot Great White Throne was named by Methodist minister Frederick Vining Fisher during a visit to Zion Canyon in 1916; Fisher remarked to his party: "Boys, I have looked for this mountain all my life, but I never expected to find it in this world. This mountain is the Great White Throne." Scout the road between the Weeping Rock and Big Bend pullouts to see which view works best for you to photograph the Great White Throne during mid- to late afternoon. Or scramble up to Angels Landing (see p. 47). *Location:* Between Zion Lodge and Temple of Sinawava.

Stop 4: Temple of Sinawava. The 4,418-foot Temple of Sinawava was named after the Paiute wolf god, Shinna'wav. It stands at the mouth of the North Fork of the Virgin River and leads to Zion Narrows (see p. 48). Midmorning and mid- to late afternoon are often best. *Location:* Northern end of Zion Canyon Scenic Drive.

Stop 5: The Watchman. A descriptive name, The Watchman is 6,545 feet high and stands at the mouth of Zion Canyon overlooking the confluence of the East and North Forks of the Virgin River. Late afternoon is best. You can photograph The Watchman from various points, including the Human History Museum, South Campground, and the pullout outside the Entrance Station. *Location:* South entrance to Zion National Park.

Palisades, East Temple,
Zion–Mt. Carmel Highway

Zion–Mt. Carmel Highway (9)

The Vista: Arguably one of the most scenic and breathtaking highways in the West, the Zion–Mt. Carmel Highway was built in 1930. Writer Angus M. Woodbury called it "one of the most spectacular engineering feats in the history of road-building." Zion–Mt. Carmel Highway traces

Directions: From the Zion Canyon Visitor Center, drive 1.1 miles north to Zion–Mt. Carmel Highway, turn right (east), and drive up the switchbacks toward the lower tunnel entrance. Pullouts before and after each of the six hairpin turns offer photographic vistas.
The Hikes: Curbside strolls. Also, the 1-mile Canyon Overlook Trail (160-foot climb) offers a spectacular panorama.
Natural Hazards: Traffic. Drive, pull out, and park with care, safety, and courtesy.
Neighboring Camera Stops: Zion Canyon Scenic Drive

the course of Pine Creek from 6,670-foot Checkerboard Mesa to the confluence of the North Fork of the Virgin River in Zion Canyon. Dangerously beautiful, it takes a concerted effort to keep your eyes on the narrow, winding road as it switchbacks through gallery-windowed tunnels, down the precipitous cliffs of 6,803-foot Bridge Mountain beneath the imposing walls of 7,709-foot East Temple. Numerous pullouts below the mile-long tunnel offer neck-craning visitors the opportunity to pull over and photograph the extraordinary scenery safely.

Photography: Whether you've pitched your tent in the South Campground or bedded down at a nearby lodge, take time to scout the pullouts between the lower tunnel entrance and the junction of Zion–Mt. Carmel Highway and Zion Canyon Scenic Drive. Both early morning and late afternoon offer opportunities to photograph the stupendous cliffs and crags of Bridge Mountain and East Temple from pullouts along the highway.

Angels Landing (10)

The Vista: Perched 1,500 feet above the valley floor, 5,790-foot Angels Landing offers a raptor's view of Zion Narrows to the north and the breadth of Zion Canyon to the south. Gaze in almost any other direction as well, and the landmarks offer stunning views to photograph and unique stories to tell. To the northeast is 6,505-foot Observation Point. When Leo A. Snow surveyed Zion Canyon in 1908, he climbed all the way up to the East Rim and used Observation Point as a triangulation station. Describing the vista, Snow wrote: "A view can be had of this canyon surpassed only by a similar view of the Grand Canyon of the Colorado River. At intervals along the west side of the canyon, streams of various sizes rush over the edge of the chasm, forming waterfalls 800 to 2000 feet high." East of Angels Landing sits 6,496-foot Cable Mountain. Faced with a shortage of lumber to build log cabins, settlers turned to David Flannigan, who developed a cable system in 1906 to lower timber from the summit of Cable Mountain nearly 2,000 feet to Zion Canyon. Standing on the edge of Angels Landing, one can only imagine a daring teenage boy riding atop a cabled stack of yellow pine from Cable Mountain to the bottom of the canyon. And that's what Quinby Stewart did in 1910 on a bet to eat his fill of watermelon at the foot of the cliff 1,800 feet below. Southeast of Angels Landing you can see the 6,744-foot Great White Throne. In 1967 Yosemite climbers Fred Becky, Pat Callis, and the late Galen Rowell—a renowned wilderness photographer—made Zion Canyon's first big wall ascent by scaling its 2,200-foot sandstone face that sometimes crumbled like "brown sugar."

Leading from the North Fork of the Virgin River to an aerie of rock 1,500 feet above, the trail to Angels Landing was built in 1926. It was no mean feat. Chiseled and blasted into solid rock, the headwall of Refrigerator Canyon had to be gouged with 21 switchbacks that were so narrow that old timers said, "It is the only place in the world you can see both ends of a horse at the same time." Named Walter's Wiggles after Zion caretaker Walter Ruesch, the switchbacks top out at 600 feet above on a ledge of rock called Scout Lookout. It is the last piece of flat ground to stand on before you scramble up the craggy knife edge to Angels Landing. A half-mile-long section of chain, hand-polished by years of white-knuckle use,

---

Directions: From the Zion Canyon Visitor Center, take the shuttle (in season), or drive (off-season) 3 miles up Zion Canyon Scenic Drive to the Grotto

Day Hike Only: Largely paved, the steep, potholed 2½-mile-long trail climbs 1,510 vertical feet and follows the West Rim Trail through Refrigerator Canyon to Walter's Wiggles, a series of 21 switchbacks that leads to Scouts Lookout. A heavy chain tenuously links the exposed half-mile ridgeline between Scout Lookout and Angels Landing.

Natural Hazards: Lightning during monsoons, ice during winter, and exposure—yikes!—all year long

Map (optional): USGS 7.5-minute map: Temple of Sinawava, Utah

offers some protection from the yawning drop.

Photography: If you're carrying a large-format camera, you may find it safer to set up your tripod below Angels Landing at Scout Lookout. Early morning and late afternoon are best.

Zion Narrows (11)

The Vista: Draining the heights of the 8,500-foot Kolob Plateau, the North Fork of the Virgin River—together with Deep Creek, Kolob Creek, Goose Creek, and Orderville Canyon—has carved a 16-mile-

The Narrows, Zion National Park

long narrow canyon through the 2,200-foot thick Navajo sandstone. Plummeting 76 feet per mile, the North Fork of the Virgin River has created one of the most beautiful and renowned canyons in the West. Hanging gardens, white cascades, and sweet-water springs adorn the ver-

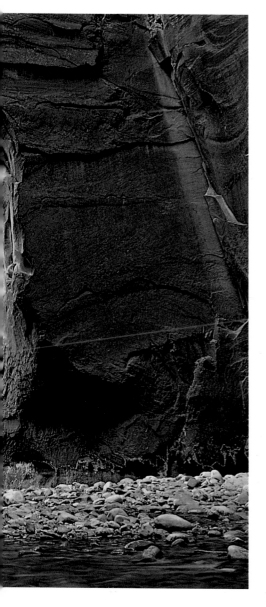

dant, serpentine course of Zion Narrows as it twists and turns beneath overhanging alcoves and looming cliffs that pinch out the sun. For the Parrusits band of Paiute it was a place of reverence. They called the canyon *I-u-goone*, "like an arrow quiver," because they believed there was only one way into and one way out of it. The river was known as *Mukun'tuweap*, "straight canyon stream." Their benevolent spirit Wai-no-pits inhabited the shadows of Zion Narrows. The feared Wolf god Shinna'wav guarded the entrance.

Few early explorers had reason to visit such a mysterious and daunting chasm until Mormon missionary Jacob Hamblin led Major John Wesley Powell into the area in 1870. After two exhausting days of struggling through quicksand and wading and half-swimming down the East Fork of the Virgin River through *Pa-ru-nu-weap* ("roaring water") Canyon, Powell was determined to explore the North Fork of the Virgin River. Striking out from the settlement of Schunesburg on September 12, Powell made the first known exploration of Zion Narrows to its headwaters. He wrote: "Entering this, we were compelled to wade upstream; the water filled the entire channel. . . . The walls . . . are vertical for a thousand feet or more. . . . Everywhere as we went we found springs bursting out at the foot of the walls."

When John K. Hillers photographed Zion Canyon in 1872, his words painted a similar scene. On April 8 he wrote: "The scenery is grand for its kind and affords fine subjects for the camera. . . . Pinnacles innumerable, forming an immense harrow upside down. Here and there are scattered peaks, overlooking the others by a thousand feet, or like giants among dwarfs. All bare rocks, no vegetation on the towers. Camped near a little seep spring."

Photography: Barring crowds, this short, spectacular canyoneering journey is a wonderful photographic trek. Slippery footing demands that you pay attention to where you're walking, so stop before, during, and after stream crossings to eyeball the scenery around you.

Directions: To day hike up Zion Narrows, take the park shuttle (in season), or drive (off season) from the Zion Canyon Visitor Center to the Riverside Walk trailhead. You can also day hike the length of Zion Narrows from top to bottom, but to photograph it properly, you should spend at least two days and a night backpacking through the canyon. To through hike from top to bottom, you need to use a shuttle vehicle. Drive 12.3 miles up the Zion–Mt. Carmel Highway to the Chamberlain Ranch Road turnoff, turn left, and drive 16.7 miles north on the dirt road to Chamberlain Ranch trailhead. You may find it easier to use a commercial shuttle (see info at right).

The Trek: 16 miles downstream (elevation loss, 1,245 vertical feet). Downstream traveling time: Figure 1 to 2 miles an hour, depending on water depth, footing, and obstacles.

Mileposts and Elevations (±):

Mile 0.0: Chamberlain Ranch trailhead (6,150 feet)

Mile 3.0: Bulloch Cabin (5,785 feet)

Mile 5.8: Upper Narrows (5,600 feet)

Mile 8.6: Falls (15 feet high)

Mile 9.0: Deep Creek (5,020 feet): Enters from northwest (river right, facing downstream)

Mile 9.5: Kolob Creek: Enters from northwest (river right)

Mile 10.5: Goose Creek: Enters from northwest (river right)

Mile 11.0: Big Springs (4,815 feet): On west wall (river right)

Mile 12.0: Zion Narrows

Mile 13.3: Orderville Canyon, 4,635 feet: Enters from east (river left)

Mile 14.5: Mystery Canyon Falls (120 feet high): On east wall (river left)

Mile 16.0: Temple of Sinawava (4,471 feet)

Natural Hazards: Flash floods, hypothermia, slippery footing, and deep pools of water throughout, including the confluences of Deep Creek, Kolob Creek, Goose Creek, and Orderville Canyon

Contact: For backcountry information, phone 435-772-0170, or visit www.nps.gov/zion

Backcountry Fees and Permits: Required for all overnight hikes and through day hikes of Zion Narrows, Left Fork of North Creek, Kolob Creek, and others. Fees are $10 for 1–2 hikers, $15 for 3–7 hikers, and $20 for 8–12 hikers.

Commercial Shuttles: Available for through hikes of Zion Narrows. Phone 435-772-1001, or visit www.zionadventures.com.

Maps (required): USGS 7.5-minute maps: Temple of Sinawava, and Straight Canyon, Utah

Neighboring Camera Stops: Zion–Mt. Carmel Highway

Season: May through October, depending on runoff and weather

V. Capitol Reef National Park

The Story Behind the Scenery: Slashing across the landscape for a hundred miles from north to south, Waterpocket Fold divides southern Utah in half. This spectacular double reef of rock soars a half mile above the crimson desert and reaches heights of 7,355 feet. Waterpocket Fold was formed 60 million years ago during an uplift of the Colorado Plateau, when tectonic plates collided, forcing one sedimentary rock layer over the other. The resulting upthrust, or monocline, created an upheaval of brilliantly colored domes, alcoves, monoliths, arches, and gorges in one of the least explored regions of the contiguous United States. Waterpocket Fold is mesmerizing to the naked eye, with few lines of weakness breaching this nearly impenetrable barrier of serrated, multicolored sedimentary rock that stands between 10,908-foot Boulder Mountain to the west and 11,371-foot Henry Mountain to the east. Carved over many millennia by violent flash floods, relentless wind sheer, and thundering rockfall, deep, serpentine gorges offered the only passages through an ancient and formidable landmark the Paiute accurately named *Timpi-avić*, "Rock Mountain." It was the place the Southern Paiute were said to rarely venture through, and it formed the geographical boundary between their homelands on the west side of Waterpocket Fold and those of the Ute who lived on the east.

Long said to be called the "Land of the Sleeping Rainbow" by the Navajo (although I couldn't verify this popular reference in the lexicons of Navajo place-names), this rugged no-man's-land is traversed by only a handful of gorges—and these made for difficult travel. Sluicing through Waterpocket Fold on the north is the Fremont River. Between A.D. 700 and 1250, the *Mukwic* (ancestral Paiute and Ute) used this life-saving watercourse that had chiseled a verdant chasm through flying buttresses and towering walls of Navajo Sandstone. The Mukwic, or perhaps Archaic hunters and gatherers long before them, carved horned medicine men in the slickrock walls that can still be seen near the head of the Fremont River.

During the summer of 1872, Powell's men picked up the Mukwic's ancient trail on a tributary of the Fremont River called Tantalus Creek. Under the leadership of surveyor Almon Harris Thompson, photographers James Fennemore and John K. Hillers, artist Frederick S. Dellenbaugh, and five other topographers, packers, and assistants made the first recorded crossing of Waterpocket Fold. After discovering the Escalante River, the expedition continued east on horseback into unchartered territory in search of the Dirty Devil River. Tracing Thompson's official report and diary notes across the shaded contours of modern topographical maps from the Escalante River to Capitol Reef National Park, Powell's men named and then followed Pleasant Creek east from Boulder Mountain into the rugged recesses of Waterpocket Fold. On June 13 Thompson described the untamed character of the country: "The land was desolate and dry, and exactly as the region appeared from above, a complete labyrinth of variously

Wolfs Tooth, Hickman Bridge, Capitol Reef National Park

coloured [sic] cliffs and canyons." Emerging from this labyrinth of barren rock on the east side of Waterpocket Fold, Hillers photographed a narrow, boulder-choked tributary of the Fremont River named Tantalus Creek. Expedition members later climbed to the summit of the Henry Mountains, and 15 days after leaving Kanab, they finally found the Dirty Devil River. Thompson described what largely remains terra incognita for modern visitors and photographers: "The distance traveled by the main party, to the mouth of the Dirty Devil River, was two hundred and eighty miles, through a country, for the most part, completely unknown. I have not been able to find any evidence that white men ever before visited any considerable portion of the country explored." When the expedition reached the mouth of the Dirty Devil River on June 22, they spent two days caulking the Cañonita, the boat that had been cached during their journey down the Green and Colorado Rivers nine months earlier. Thompson retraced their cross-country route back to the expedition outpost at Kanab, and Hillers, Fennemore, Dellenbaugh and crew ran the Colorado River to winter camp at Lees Ferry. Equipped with pencils, oil paints, watercolors, and photographic glass plates, expedition photographers, artists, and diarists were greeted by a dazzling rainbow of stone as they recorded their passage through Glen Canyon.

You can retrace all or parts of the Powell Expedition's route from Kanab, Utah, to the confluence of the Dirty Devil and Colorado Rivers by pickup truck via scenic and back roads, by raft via the Colorado River, and by foot and horseback via historic routes and trails. Or you can backpack all or sections of the 812-mile-long Hayduke Trail from Zion National Park, across Capitol Reef National Park, to Arches National Park (see "Trip & Expedition Planner"). Either way, you'll be struck by Waterpocket Fold's vibrant colors and brilliant shades of reds, whites, buffs, cinnamon browns, yellows, greens, and oranges that comprise a geological palette of Wingate sandstone, Navajo sandstone, Chinle, Moenkopi, and Dakota formations and Shinarump conglomerate.

First Photographed: John K. Hillers took the first-known photograph of Waterpocket Fold between June 12th and 14th, 1872. Hillers's photograph of Tantalus Creek was reproduced in Dellenbaugh's 1908 book, *A Canyon Voyage*. In comparing Dellenbaugh's name and description, there's a fair possibility that his "Tantalus Creek" may be the Tarantula Creek that appears on modern topographical maps.

Photography: Many of Capitol Reef National Park's colorful icons can be photographed from paved scenic roads. Day hikes and rugged backpacks lead through slickrock canyons, and across the rimrock, to scenic vistas throughout the length of Waterpocket Fold.

Stops and Viewpoints

Utah Highway 24 West: The 11-mile stretch of highway heads east from Torrey to the Capitol Reef Visitor Center and offers a colorful spectrum of geological formations and panoramas that are best photographed in late afternoon. From west to east, the scenic pullouts include Twin Rocks, Chimney Rock, Panorama Point, and the Castle, Capitol Reef's icon. Be sure to drive the dirt road from

Directions: From Bryce National Park, Utah, drive 46 miles on UT 12 to Escalante and then another 13 miles north to Boulder. This cliff-hugging 13-mile stretch of highway crosses the Hogback and is one of the Colorado Plateau's most scenic and breathtaking roads. Milepost 78 makes a safe pullout to photograph the view during early morning and late afternoon. From Boulder, continue 73 miles north on UT 12 to Torrey, turn east on UT 24, and drive 11 miles to the Capitol Reef Visitor Center.

The Hikes: Curbside strolls, ½-mile Goosenecks Trail (easy climb), 3½-mile Chimney Rock Trail (500-foot climb), and others. Ask for the free Capitol Reef trail guide at the visitor center.

Natural Hazards: Heat during summer; lightning on the rimrock and flash floods in the canyons and arroyos during monsoons. Park Rangers often close Scenic Drive, Grand Wash, and Capitol Gorge on short notice when local storm cells heighten flash flood danger.

Contact: Phone 435-425-3791, or visit www.nps.gov/care

Entrance Fee: $5 per car for seven days or National Parks Pass

Campground Fee: Fruita Campground, $10 per night

Backcountry Permits: Required for overnight backpacking. No fee.

Maps (optional): USGS 7.5-minute maps: Twin Rocks, Fruita, and Golden Throne, Utah

Neighboring Camera Stops: Bryce Canyon National Park, Utah

Season: All year

Capitol Reef Natural History Association: Phone 435-425-3791, ext. 113 or 115

Panorama Point to the Goosenecks Overlook to scout the deep serpentine fissure of Sulphur Creek.

Utah Highway 24 East: The 9-mile stretch of highway heads east from the Capitol Reef Visitor Center to Observation Point and traces the winding course of the Fremont River beneath magnificent walls and domes of Navajo sandstone that are best photographed in early morning and late afternoon. West to east, the scenic pullouts include Historic Fruita School, Fremont River petroglyphs, Hickman Bridge trailhead, Behunin Cabin, and others. Be sure to walk the short wooden footbridge along the Fremont River and listen to the music of running water echoing through the high desert.

Scenic Drive: The paved 10-mile Scenic Drive heads south from the Capitol Reef Visitor Center to Capitol Gorge and roller-coasters beneath the castellated walls of Waterpocket Fold. North to south, the scenic vistas on the left (east) side of the road include the unnamed, striated towers of Moenkopi Shale, sinister-looking Evil Rock near Grand Wash, the Great Curtain at Slickrock Divide, the Egyptian Temple, the North Portal of Capitol Gorge, and the rugged back road through South Draw. Be sure to ask for the free Scenic Drive guide at the visitor center.

Hickman Bridge (12)

The Vista: Spanning 133 feet, Hickman Bridge stands 125 feet above the steep canyon floor. The natural bridge of Kayenta sandstone was named in honor of 1920s park proponent Joseph S. Hickman, who led the effort to protect Waterpocket Fold. Hickman's efforts, and those of others, paid off when President Franklin D. Roosevelt established Capitol Reef National Monument on August 2, 1937. It was designated a national park in 1971. Tucked in the shadows beneath the western rimrock, Hickman Bridge can be difficult to photograph in late afternoon. So scout it in early morning and late afternoon to see what works best for you. Bring a graduated neutral-density filter to expose for sunlight and shadow during late afternoon light.

A superior view to Hickman Bridge, I think, is what I call Wolfs Tooth. As the Hickman Bridge trail tops out on the rimrock overlooking the Fremont River Gorge, look due south at the pyramid of Navajo sandstone surrounded by white domes and fossilized sand dunes. Early morning and late afternoon are best to photograph the view of Wolfs Tooth.

> **Directions:** From the Capitol Reef Visitor Center, drive 1.75 miles east on UT 24 to the Hickman Bridge trailhead on the north side of the highway
> **The Hike:** 2 miles round-trip (400-foot climb)
> **Neighboring Camera Stops:** Fremont River Gorge
> **Map (optional):** USGS 7.5 minute map: Fruita, Utah

Grand Wash Narrows (13)

The Vista: Grand Wash is one of six principal canyons that provided passage across Waterpocket Fold for Native Americans, explorers, pioneers, and bandits. North to south, they include Fremont River Gorge, Grand Wash, Capitol Gorge, Sheets Gulch, Pleasant Creek, and Muley Twist. Located near the northern end of Capitol Reef, Grand Wash was a historic route for cowboys driving cattle between summer and winter ranges. If you've been jaded by the luminescent light of Lower Antelope Canyon and Buckskin Gulch, Grand Wash Narrows does not compare. But it does offer some midmorning possibilities if you're waiting to photograph another late-afternoon vista. The solution pockets near the head of the canyon are one good bet. Rain and snowmelt have

> **Directions:** From the Capitol Reef Visitor Center, drive 3 miles south on Scenic Drive to the Grand Wash turnoff. Turn left, and drive ½ mile east on the dirt road to an unmarked pullout on the right (south) side of the road to reach the mouth of Shinob Canyon; or drive 1½ miles northeast from Scenic Drive to reach the Grand Wash Narrows trailhead.
> **The Hike:** Shinob Canyon, ½ mile round-trip (cross-country, along the streambed); Grand Wash Narrows, 4 miles round-trip (cross-country, along the streambed)
> **Neighboring Camera Stops:** Capitol Gorge
> **Map (optional):** USGS 7.5-Minute map: Fruita, Utah

Solution Pockets, Grand Wash Narrows, Capitol Reef National Park

dissolved the porous Wingate sandstone to create captivating hollows that make fine detail photographs.

In my opinion, a more enticing destination nearby is Shinob Canyon. A short tributary of Grand Wash, Shinob Canyon takes its name from Shinob, "the second great god" of the Paiute, and the younger brother of Tobats, who created the world. Near the head of this canyon, a towering pillar of stone on the west wall can be photographed when the sun winks over the rimrock during midmorning. Look for the pioneer inscription on the east wall above the wash: A.E. HANKS NOTÒM FEB. 21ST, 1905.

Capitol Gorge (14)

The Vista: In 1884 Mormon pioneer Elijah Cutler Behunin drove the first wagon through the rugged, flashflood-scoured course of Captitol Gorge across Waterpocket Fold. Little did Behunin know at the time, but Capitol Gorge would soon become the gateway to the "Outlaw Empire." Lead by Utah native Robert Leroy Parker, "Butch Cassidy," and Harry Longabaugh, "the Sundance Kid," the Wild Bunch used Capitol Gorge during the 1890s to reach Circle Valley from their hideout at Robbers Roost in the San Rafael Swell. This legendary horse-thief trail, immortalized in the Paul Newman and Robert Redford movie *Butch Cassidy and the Sundance Kid,*

Directions: From the Capitol Reef Visitor Center, drive 10 miles south on Scenic Drive to the Capitol Gorge turnoff. Turn left, and drive 2 miles east on the dirt road to the trailhead.

The Hike: 2 miles round-trip to the Tanks (cross-country, along the streambed)

Neighboring Camera Stops: Grand Wash Narrows and Shinob Canyon

Map (optional): USGS 7.5-minute map: Golden Throne, Utah

leads beneath 1,200-foot-high walls of Wingate sandstone. Prospectors and settlers left their marks alongside ancient petroglyphs when, in 1871, they began the practice of inscribing their names in "pioneer registers" in Capitol Gorge.

The Curtain, Capitol Gorge, Capitol Reef National Park

The Sentinel, Bryce Canyon National Park

VI. Bryce Canyon National Park

The Story Behind the Scenery: When Scottish immigrant Ebenezer Bryce homesteaded 200 acres near the mouth of Bryce Canyon in 1875, he said, "It's a hell of a place to lose a cow." The Mormon pioneer was talking about the maze of hoodoos he tracked maverick cattle through. Ebenezer and his wife, Mary, put down stakes at the foot of the Pink Cliffs, and the settlement of Tropic sprang up along the fertile banks of the Paria River. Sixty-five million years earlier a large inland lake covered southwestern Utah. Over the millennia the water evaporated, depositing a brilliant geological layer called the Claron Formation. As the region's plateaus began uplifting and faulting 10 to15 millions years ago, the Claron Formation weathered and eroded, producing the colorful hoodoos that Bryce Canyon became famous for.

First described by the Paiute, who named it *Paunsaganti* ("Beaver Place"), John Wesley Powell's men first saw the Pink Cliffs of the Paunsaugunt Plateau while surveying the high plateaus north of Kanab during 1871–72: "North of our camp, and eight miles distant, the south end of the table land [sic] known as the Pauns-a'-gunt Plateau rose to an altitude which we determined to be 3,295 feet above our camp, or about nine thousand two hundred feet above our camp." When surveyor and topographer Almon Harris Thompson wrote those words he was looking in the direction of 9,105-foot Rainbow Point on the southern end of the Paunsaugunt Plateau, and his elevation estimate was only off by 95 feet! Thomp-

Natural Bridge, Bryce Canyon National Park

son continued: "These cliffs show in the distance a beautiful pink color, and, for the upper 2,000 feet, present bold, perpendicular faces, with here and there steep, rocky slopes." Others, like expedition artist Frederick S. Dellenbaugh, set the stage for future writers and described the Pink Cliffs in more glowing terms: "Emerging from the forest of pine and cedar we saw again the magnificent, kaleidoscopic cliff country lying to the north . . . the broken meandering face of the Pink Cliffs, frosted with snow. . . . A more extraordinary, bewildering landscape, both as to form and colour [sic], could hardly be found in all the world." Word traveled, as did Jack Hillers's photographs of the Pink Cliffs.

Little more than two decades after a severe drought drove Ebenezer Bryce out of the weird and beautiful country that still bears his name, President Warren G. Harding established Bryce Canyon National Monument on June 8, 1923. A mere 18 miles long, 5 miles wide, and 800 feet deep, Bryce Canyon National Park does not compare to the Grand Canyon's stature. But the 35,835-acre national park was established in 1924 to protect what U.S. Deputy Surveyor T. C. Bailey in 1876 first said was: "One of the wonders of the world. . . . There are thousands of red, white, purple, and vermilion colored rocks . . . presenting the wildest and most wonderful scene that the eye of man ever beheld."

First Photographed: John K. Hillers took the first-known photographs of the region on June 2, 1872. Hillers's prose captures the moment when adventure, discovery, and art coalesce: "Climbed up on a narrow strip resembling a hogback, from bottom to top 2500 feet—in some places it was only $2\frac{1}{2}$ feet wide on the top. The sun was just going down. When I reached the top I stopped to breathe. I looked down the awful chasm—it looked wild and forbidden, the valley below in deep shadow. Table Mountain north of it with its pink colors reflected back the golden light of the setting sun long after she had gone from my view. A wilder view I never beheld. It surpassed the Wild Scene [sic] on the Colorado [River] at Lava Falls. What a picture for Burstadt [Bierstadt]." Hillers's photograph of the Pink Cliffs was reproduced in Dellenbaugh's 1902 book, *The Romance of The Colorado River.*

Photography: Most of Bryce Canyon's scenic vistas and destinations are located on or below the East Rim of the Paunsaugunt Plateau. As a result, morning light is often the best and most reliable time for scenic photography. During peak afternoon light, many of these vistas and destinations are either completely in shadow or, much like the plaza of a bullring, split with a receding horizontal line of sunlight fading to shadow. To expose for sunlight and shadow during the late afternoon, use a graduated neutral-density filter. Depending on the season and the angle of the sun, I sometimes wait until twilight to get optimum results at day's end. Locals claim Bryce Canyon has the clearest skies in the region, and stargazing park rangers attest that "7,500 [stars] are visible to the unaided eye!"

The Fairyland (15)

The Vista: Standing on the edge of 7,758-foot Fairyland Point, the 10,158-foot Table Cliffs and Aquarius Plateau are the most recognizable landmarks on the horizon. Lit by the late-afternoon summer sun or blanketed with winter snow, they form a postcard backdrop for the Pink Cliffs, 7,405-foot Sinking Ship, and Boat Mesa. Look beneath your feet, though, and your imagination will run wild. Walk along the rim, change angles, and the Fairyland's hoodoos look like totems of reptiles peering at the sun, moon, and sky. To others, they look like gnomes, goblins, and ghosts. In 1936 a man named "Indian Dick" told park rangers that Bryce Canyon's hoodoos and stone faces were Paiute ancestors turned to stone. "For some reason the Legend People in that place were bad," Indian Dick said. "Because they were bad, Coyote turned them all into rocks. You can see [them] in that place now, all turned into rocks; some standing in rows, some sitting down, some holding onto others. You can see their faces, with paint on them, just as

---

Directions: From the Bryce Canyon Visitor Center, drive 1 mile north to the turnoff for the Fairyland, then 1 mile farther to Fairyland Point

The Hikes: Rim walks of your choice. Rim Trail south to 8,015-foot Sunrise Point, $2\frac{1}{2}$-miles one way; Fairyland Loop Trail, 8 miles, (900-foot climb).

Neighboring Camera Stops: Sunrise Point

Map (optional): USGS 7.5-minute map: Bryce Canyon, Utah

The Fairyland, Bryce Canyon National Park

they were before they became rocks." The Fairyland best fits the Paiute elder's description.

However you interpret these strange and wonderful hoodoos, they stand alone in the viewfinder. Though, from the postcards I've seen, many photographers simply use them as foreground.

Sunset Point (16)

The Vista: Overlooking Bryce Amphitheater, 7,999-foot Sunset Point offers one of the best *sunrise* views in Bryce Canyon National Park. From Clarence E. Dutton's description of the Pink Cliffs in his 1880 *Report on the Geology of the High Plateaus of Utah,* it sounds like he was describing the view from Sunset Point: "Standing obelisks, prostrate columns, shattered capitals...all bring vividly before the mind suggestions of the work of giant hands, a race of genii now chained up in a spell of enchantment, while their structures are falling in ruins through centuries of decay." From the Temple of Osiris to Three Wise Men, mythical names abound to describe Bryce Canyon's unearthly looking hoodoos. Walk several switchbacks beneath the east rim of Bryce

Directions: From the Bryce Canyon Visitor Center, drive 1.5 miles south to the turnoff for Sunset Point, and a quarter mile farther to 7,999-foot Sunset Point

The Hikes: Rim walks of your choice. Rim Trail north to Sunrise Point, ½ mile one way; Rim Trail south to 8,143-foot Inspiration Point, ¾ mile one way; and Navajo Loop Trail via Wall Street, 1¼ miles (500-foot climb).

Neighboring Camera Stops: 8,294-foot Bryce Point

Map (optional): USGS 7.5 minute map: Bryce Point, Utah

Point, and you'll see the two-eyed Mask, Thor's Hammer—named for the Norse god of thunder—and The Sentinel. A common name used throughout the West to describe rock formations that appear to

The Mask, Sunset Point, Bryce Canyon National Park

stand guard over adjoining topographical features, The Sentinel stands watch over the minarets and turrets of Bryce Amphitheater. Plunge down the short, steep switchbacks beyond, and you'll see the towering 400-year-old Douglas fir growing up from the depths of Wall Street, one of Bryce Canyon's iconic photographs. Return to the rim, and look south from Bryce Point. At either first or last light, you'll be mesmerized by the hundreds of goblins that make up Silent City standing beneath the Pink Cliffs of 8,316-foot Inspiration Point. In ideal light it's difficult to take a bad photograph of Bryce Amphitheater. It's also difficult to take an original composition unless you listen to your heart. And there are few better places to do that in Bryce Canyon National Park than at Sunset Point.

Monsoon sunrise, Bryce Point, Bryce Canyon National Park

Bryce Point (17)

The Vista: At 8,294 feet above sea level, Bryce Point offers an unforgettable panorama of sunrise over the dark-blue tablelands of the 7,040-foot Kaiparowits Plateau. Between you and there, your eye is drawn to many formations that are open to your interpretation, including the Alligator—if you can find it in the maze of hoodoos. Due north from Bryce Point are the rosette breaks and badlands that typify the Pink Cliffs. Morning light ignites these castles of rock. One of the more remarkable formations seen due west from this vista is the Wall of Windows. Where early travelers once envisioned the Basilica of Constantine, it's not difficult to imagine it being the ancient home of cliff-dwelling Mukwic of the Anaasází.

Directions: From the Visitor Center, drive 2 miles south to the Bryce Point turnoff (1.25 miles south of the Sunset Point turnoff), then 2 miles farther to Bryce Point

The Hikes: Rim walks of your choice. Rim Trail north to 8,143-foot Inspiration Point, 1½ miles one way; Peekaboo Loop Trail, 5½ miles (800-foot climb); and Under the Rim Trail south to 9,105-foot Rainbow Point, 11½ miles one way (1,500-foot climb).

Neighboring Camera Stops: Paria View and Inspiration Point

Map (optional): USGS 7.5 minute map: Bryce Point

Natural Bridge (18)

The Vista: Standing 125 feet above Bridge Canyon, Natural Bridge spans 85 feet. Mistakenly named a bridge, geologists argued that Natural Bridge is really an arch because it was originally sculpted by rain and "freeze-thaw" erosion, not by the running water that now cascades beneath it during summer monsoons. Historic black-and-white photographs of Bryce Canyon tourists show that the summit of this fragile bridge was once a popular, if precarious, destination. Resist the temptation; it is now off limits. Like Paria View's slender hand of rock, Natural Bridge can stand alone in your viewfinder, or it can be used as foreground to the forested depths of Bridge Canyon and nearby 7,833-foot Deer Mountain. Natural Bridge is well lit in mid- to late afternoon and glistens with vibrant colors after summer rains.

Directions: From the Bryce Canyon Visitor Center, drive 11 miles south to the 8,600-foot (±) Natural Bridge pullout (9 miles south of the Paria View turnoff)

The Hike: Curbside stroll

Neighboring Camera Stops: 9,105-foot Rainbow Point, 5 miles south

Map (optional): USGS 7.5-minute map: Tropic Reservoir, Utah

Paria View (19)

The Vista: Look toward the eastern horizon, and you can make out the rocky, pearl-hued bluffs of the White Cliffs. From its headwaters near 8,176-foot Paria View, the Paria River drains 935 square miles, cuts through the distant White Cliffs, and empties into the Colorado River 90 miles and 5,059 feet below your feet. Eons of runoff from the wooded highlands of the Paunsaugunt Plateau, Aquarius Plateau, and the Kaiparowits Plateau formed the Paria River, which carved one of the narrowest and most beautiful canyons on earth: the 42-mile-long, 3,233-foot-deep Buckskin Gulch/Paria Canyon.

Directly in front of you is a spectacular knife-edged monument that bares a striking resemblance to the freestanding temples of the Grand Canyon. This delicate hand of rock stands alone in your viewfinder or serves as foreground for a wide-angle photograph of the 500-foot-deep forested canyon below it and the White Cliffs beyond.

Directions: From the Bryce Canyon Visitor Center, drive 2 miles south to the Paria View turnoff (1.25 miles south of the Sunset Point turnoff), then 2 miles farther to 8,176-foot Paria View

The Hike: Curbside stroll

Photo Tip: This is a late-afternoon or twilight photograph. A neutral-density filter is a must for late-afternoon photographs.

Neighboring Camera Stops: 8,296-foot Bryce Point

Map (optional): USGS 7.5-minute map: Bryce Point, Utah

Paria View, Bryce Canyon National Park

VII. Canyonlands National Park

The Story Behind the Scenery: Ranging from deep, desert river chasms to lofty piñon- and juniper-covered mesas, Canyonlands is a primeval wilderness of stone that was home to ancient nomads who roamed the rimrock and slickrock canyons on an unending quest for food and water almost 9,000 years ago. How these Archaic hunters and gatherers survived in such a hostile and beautiful canyon environment remains largely a mystery. Cliff dwellings and archaeological remains dating between A.D. 900 and 1250 indicate the Anaasází established a tenuous toehold in what most explorers, cowboys, and uranium hunters later discovered was tortured ground. During his maiden voyage down the Green and Colorado Rivers in 1869, one-armed explorer Major John Wesley Powell climbed up from the confluence on July 19 to survey the land with expedition member George Bradley; Powell wrote: "Wherever we look there is but a wilderness of rocks—deep gorges where the rivers are lost below cliffs and towers and pinnacles, and ten thousand strangely carved forms in every direction."

Formed during an uplift of the Colorado Plateau 15 million years ago, the Green and Colorado Rivers carved Canyonlands into three ruggedly spectacular regions, each distinct from the next, each one cut off from the other by soaring precipices and sheer-walled river corridors. Island in the Sky is an arid 6,240-foot-high plateau that looms 2,000 feet above the landscape. Stand on the edge of the rimrock, and you can see the Meanders of the Colorado River to the east and

Contact: For private permits, fees, tow outs, and a list of licensed river outfitters, phone 435-719-2313, or visit www.nps.gov/cany/river
Guided Backcountry Excursions: Hiking, and 4WD trips; visit www.nps.gov/cany/guided.htm
Outdoor Education: Phone 435-719-2313, or visit www.nps.gov/cany/education
Canyonlands Natural History Association: Phone 800-840-8978, or visit www.cnha.org
Back of Beyond Books: 83 North Main, Moab, UT 84532; phone 800-700-2859, or visit www.backofbeyondbooks.com

Stillwater Canyon of the Green River to the west. At the confluence of the Green and Colorado Rivers is The Needles, a monument of fins, grabens, and arches that remain captivating to the eyes of modern visitors who roam beneath them. West of The Needles, on the opposite rim of Cataract Canyon, is The Maze, what the National Park Service brochure describes as a "thirty square mile puzzle in sandstone." It's said to be *the* most remote section of the contiguous United States. Over the horizon from The Maze is Horseshoe Canyon, a sanctuary for prehistoric canyoneers who 2,000 years ago painted one of the most remarkable galleries of life-sized pictographs in the West.

When Powell embarked on his second expedition down the Green and Colorado Rivers in 1871–72, New York photographer E. O. Beaman was hired to document the adventure. On September 18, 1871,

Beaman described the expedition's camp above Cataract Canyon's Big Drops: "For scarcely were we encamped when a sand-storm [sic] came up, so violent that, for a few minutes, it seemed as if we were to find living graves. . . . it soon passed over; and a full moon, rising clearly over the eastern crags, dispelled the grewsome [sic] shadows lurking in the cañon-walls [sic], and transformed the rapids at our feet into a caldron of phosphorescent light."

This is the mystical Canyon Country of haunting beauty that President Lyndon B. Johnson sought to protect when he established Canyonlands National Park on September 12, 1964. This is the kind of country that tugs at a photographer's soul. Be prepared for adventure and discovery.

First Photographed: E. O. Beaman took the first-known photographs of Canyonlands from the Green and Colorado Rivers in 1871. Beaman's photographs of Labyrinth, Stillwater, and Cataract Canyons were reproduced in Frederick S. Dellenbaugh's 1908 book, *A Canyon Voyage*.

Photography: One of the most exciting ways to see and photograph Canyonlands National Park is to emulate Beaman's river journey down the Colorado River through Cataract Canyon. You can launch a private river trip or embark on a commercial white-water adventure. The lazy stretches of the Green and Colorado Rivers above the confluence will not prepare you for Cataract Canyon's legendary Big Drops. April roars with big water and is great for action photography (use long-focal-length lenses), June is hot, and July–August monsoons offer spectacular lightning and waterfalls.

Dead Horse Point State Park (20)

The Vista: On the road to Island in the Sky (see p. 72), you'll see the signed turn-off to Dead Horse Point State Park. Don't pass it up. It offers one of the most spectacular and mysterious views of Canyon Country. The 5,915-foot Dead Horse Point received its name when a remuda of horses got rimrocked on the edge of the plateau during the 1800s and died of thirst 1,800 feet above the life-saving waters of the Colorado River.

Lost in the scrambled landscape of Indian Creek 15 miles due south of Dead Horse Point is an unnamed 4,905-foot butte that professor John S. Newberry climbed one insufferably hot day during the 1859 San Juan Expedition. The panorama that greeted Newberry on August 23

Directions: From Moab, Utah, drive 10 miles north on US 191 to the junction of UT 313 (22 miles south of Interstate 70). Turn left (west) on UT 313, and drive 14.5 miles to the turnoff for Dead Horse State Park.

The Hikes: Roadside strolls and rim walks

Natural Hazards: Heat during summer; lightning and flash floods during monsoons; ice and snow during winter

Contact: Phone 800-322-3770, or visit www.stateparks.utah.gov

Entrance Fee: Day use fee, $7 per vehicle

Campground Fee: $14 per night; includes entrance fee

Maps (optional): USGS 7.5-minute maps: Shafer Basin and Musselman Arch, Utah

Neighboring Camera Stops: Island in the Sky, Canyonlands National Park

Season: All year

is a fitting description of the view you'll see from Dead Horse Point: "From the pinnacle on which we stood the eye swept over an area some fifty miles in diameter, everywhere marked by . . . lofty lines of massive mesas rising in successive steps to form the frame of the picture."

In the distant eastern horizon from Dead Horse Point, you can see the lofty snow-dusted peaks of the 12,721-foot La Sal Mountains. Spanish padres Francisco Atanasio Domíguez and Silvestre Vélez de Escalante passed beneath their forested flanks during their 1776 expedition

Canyonlands and the Colorado River

to pioneer a new route from Santa Fé, New Mexico, to Monterey, California. Domínguez and Escalante first named the mountains the Sierra de la Sal for the salt they discovered at their base. The named changed to Manti La Salle Mountains during the 1800s when Domínguez and Escalante's route became more widely used and known as the Old Spanish Trail. "Manti" is an Anglicized pronunciation of the Spanish word *monte*, which means "mountain."

Look southwest from Dead Horse Point, and the silver ribbons of the Green and Colorado Rivers can be seen in ideal light. Though Cataract Canyon is recognized as the domain of Powell's 1869 and 1871–71 expeditions, a French Canadian trapper named D. Julien may have attempted running it before Powell in a crude bull hide boat during May of 1836. The Mysterious "D. Julien," as he was described by historian Charles Kelly in his 1933 journal account by that title, may have carved his name in five different locations in the walls of Stillwater, Labyrinth, and Cataract Canyons. Julien's May 3, 1836, inscription of a sunbird and boat at Hell Roaring Canyon on the Green River, signed D. JULIEN 1836 3 MAI, suggests Julien ran the Green and Colorado Rivers before disappearing from history—or drowning in Cataract Canyon.

Photography: West of Dead Horse Point Overlook, you can photograph the Gooseneck of the Colorado River between dawn and sunrise. East of the overlook you can photograph Canyon Country backdropped by the La Sal Mountains between late afternoon and twilight.

Mesa Arch, Island in the Sky, Canyonlands National Park

Island in the Sky (21)

The Vista: Assigned to survey the heart of Canyon Country to pinpoint the confluence of the Green and Colorado Rivers in 1859, Captain John N. Macomb, U.S. Army Corps of Engineers, did not foresee the colorful landscape that would greet modern visitors and tourists. In his 1876 *Report of the Exploring Expedition from Santa Fe, New Mexico, to the Junction of the Grand and Green Rivers of the Great Colorado River of the West, 1859,* Macomb wrote: "I cannot conceive of a more impracticable region than the one we now find ourselves in." The same thoughts undoubtedly crossed the minds of the ancestral Puebloans who inhabited

Island in the Sky from A.D. 900 to 1250. They hunted bighorn sheep and rabbits; gathered pine nuts; tilled corn, beans, and squash; and built isolated cliff dwellings and hidden storage granaries. Attached to Macomb's survey was Professor John S. Newberry. He described the ancient cliff dwellings they encountered during the two-and-a-half-month-long expedition: "Here the houses are built into the sides of cliffs . . . evidence that these dreadful cañons were once the homes of families belonging to that great people formerly spread over this region now so utterly sterile, solitary, and worthless."

Stand anywhere along the lofty rims of Island in the Sky or the terraces of the White Rim during midsummer when

Directions: From Moab, Utah, drive 8.5 miles north on US 191 to junction of UT 313 (20.5 miles south of Interstate 70). Turn left (west) on UT 313, and drive 22 miles to the Island in the Sky Visitor Center.

Scenic Drive: From the visitor center, the paved Canyonlands Scenic Drive leads 12 miles south across Island in the Sky to the Grandview Point Overlook. Five miles south of the visitor center, the right fork of the scenic drive leads 4.5 miles northwest to the Upheaval Dome Trailhead.

Mileposts, Viewpoints, and Elevations (±):
Mile 0.0, Stop 1: 5,945-foot Visitor Center
Mile 0.5, Stop 2: 5,900-foot Shafer Canyon Overlook
Mile 1.0, Stop 3: 5,900-foot Shafer Trail Overlook
Mile 1.2, Stop 4: 5,900-foot The Neck
Mile 1.8, Stop 5: 6,247-foot Grays Pasture
Mile 6.3, Stop 6: 6,100-foot Mesa Arch Trailhead
Mile 6.5, Stop 7: Grandview Point junction, veer left (south)
Mile 7.6, Stop 8: 6,205-foot Candlestick Tower Overlook (5,865-foot high Candlestick Tower is 450 feet tall)
Mile 9.1, Stop 9: 6,100-foot Murphy Point Trailhead
Mile 9.7, Stop 10: 6,240-foot Buck Canyon Overlook
Mile 11.5, Stop 11: 6,209-foot White Rim Overlook Trailhead
Mile 12.2, Stop 12: 6,100-foot Orange Cliffs Overlook
Mile 12.3, Stop 13: 6,080-foot Grand View Point Overlook

Upheaval Dome Junction: Begin Mile 0
Mile 0.0, Stop 1: Road Junction
Mile 0.2, Stop 2: Turnoff to Willow Flat Campground, (1 mile south) and 6,000-foot Green River Overlook (quarter mile south of campground)
Mile 0.7, Stop 3: 6,298-foot Aztec Butte View Point
Mile 2.5, Stop 4: 5,800-foot Holeman Spring Canyon Overlook
Mile 3.3, Stop 5: 5,800-foot Alcove Spring Trailhead View
Mile 3.7, Stop 6: 5,800-foot Whale Rock View Point
Mile 4.5, Stop 7: 5,800-foot Upheaval Dome Trailhead

The Hikes: Curbside strolls and rim walks. South: $1/2$-mile Mesa Arch Loop Trail (100-foot climb), $1^2/_{10}$-mile White Rim Overlook Trail and 4-mile Murphy Point Trail (100-foot climb). Northwest: 1-mile Whale Rock Trail (100-foot climb), and $1^3/_4$-mile Upheaval Dome Overlook Trail (200-foot climb).

Natural Hazards: Heat during summer; rock fall, lightning, and flash floods during monsoons; ice and snow during winter

Contact: Phone 435-259-4712, or visit www.nps.gov/cany/island

Entrance Fee: $10 per vehicle, or National Parks Pass

Campground Fee: Willow Flat, $5 per night

Backcountry Permits and Fees: Backpacking, $15 per group of five to seven people. Phone 435-259-4351, or visit www.nps.gov/cany/reserve.

Maps (optional): USGS 7.5-minute maps: Musselman Arch, Monument Basin, and Upheaval Dome, Utah

Neighboring Camera Stops: Dead Horse Point State Park

temperatures push 100 degrees in the shade of a juniper, and the sun-bleached skies, burning rimrock, and languid courses of the Green and Colorado Rivers can indeed look "sterile, solitary, and worthless." Yet it's inspiring to know that long before Canyonlands was recognized as a National Park, Native peoples, explorers, and pioneer photographers survived in such an austere and hostile environment. Journey today to any these scenic viewpoints on the far side of civilization—at dawn when the air often stands still and quiet or at twilight when up-canyon winds can roar over the rimrock—and the ambient light, colors, and panoramas will enthrall you.

Photography: If you have a high-clearance four-wheel-drive vehicle, you can photograph the world beneath the horizon line by driving the 100-mile-long White Rim Road. The three-day journey follows the sandstone terraces of the White Rim around Island in the Sky about midlevel between the plateau rim and the banks of the Colorado and Green Rivers. The White Rim Road offers intimate views of soaring cliffs, deep chasms, and towering monuments. If you're limited to a two-wheel-drive vehicle, you'll still have plenty of photo opportunities by driving the paved 16-mile Canyonlands Scenic Drive along the outer rim of Island in the Sky. Of the dozen or more viewpoints that can reached from your vehicle by roadside strolls and rim walks, 6,800-foot Mesa Arch is the most coveted by photographers. It is Island in the Sky's most distinct—and most-often photocopied—icon. All the photographs I've seen of Mesa Arch are taken from the same angle, from the southwest. The

5,400-foot-high (±) group of pinnacles a mile and a half east of Mesa Arch are Monster Tower (650 feet tall), Washer Woman Tower (400 feet tall), and Islet-in-the-Sky (400 feet tall). Backdropped by the 5,835-foot flat-topped monument of Airport Tower, they are nearly always framed through the stone eyelids of Mesa Arch at sunrise. It reminds me of something a U.S. Marine colonel told me while

North Six-shooter Peak, Newspaper Rock State Park, Canyonlands National Park

watching his charges photograph a historic grave on Arizona's *Camino del Diablo* ("Road of the Devil") during the 50th anniversary celebration of the Cabeza Prieta National Wildlife Refuge: "Don't they realize I've already taken *that* picture?" Change the angle, move to the left, and try framing Mesa Arch from the northwest—or from your own distinct perspective.

Newspaper Rock State Park (22)

The Vista: On the road to The Needles, you'll see the signed turnoff for Newspaper Rock. Don't pass it up. It has one of the most intriguing petroglyph panels in Canyon Country. Etchings by prehistoric peoples, Native Americans, Spaniards,

Directions: From Moab, Utah, drive 40 miles south on US 191 to the junction of UT 211 (14 miles north of Montecello). Turn left (west) on UT 211, and drive 10 miles to Newspaper Rock State Park. Drive 19 miles farther toward The Needles district of Canyonlands National Park until you see unmarked roadside vistas of North Six-shooter Peak.

The Hikes: Roadside strolls

Natural Hazards: Heat during summer; rockfall, lightning, and flash floods during monsoons; ice and snow during winter

Contact: Phone 435-587-1500, or visit www.blm.gov/utah/montecello/camping.htm

Entrance Fee: No fee

Campground Fee: No fee

Maps (optional): USGS 7.5-minute maps: North Six-shooter Peak, and Photograph Gap, Utah

Neighboring Camera Stops: Cave Spring, The Needles

Season: All year

and Anglos date back 2,000 years. Following the ancient migration course along Indian Creek between the Colorado River in the northwest and the 11,360-foot Abajo Mountains in the southeast, early travelers etched their dreams and calling cards in the dark-brown patina of what once was a tabula rasa of desert varnish. Footprints, wheels (or "circles of life," according to the local Ute), snakes, horned men, and horseback archers hunting elk are some of the mystifying drawings in a scenic area that was called "Photograph Gap" long before the U.S. Geological topographical map *Photograph Gap, Utah,* was published in 1987.

Follow the narrow highway beneath the rimrock along the banks of Indian Creek northwest until 6,132-foot South Six-shooter Peak and 6,379-foot North Six-shooter Peak come into view. When the Macomb Expedition followed this route in 1859, the *Map of Utah Territory* called this no-man's-land "Region Unexplored Scientifically." One of John S. Newberry's sketches that illustrate Macomb's official report includes both of these striking peaks. Homesteaded between 1929 and 1942 by a hundred-member religious sect called the "Home of Truth," Indian Creek was discovered by rock climbers during the 1960s. The 300-foot-tall North Six-shooter Peak was first climbed on August 14, 1962, and the 175-foot-tall South Six-shooter Peak was later scaled in September 1969. Enticing to climbers, both peaks are magical settings for photographers during full moons.

Photography: You can photograph Newspaper Rock in the shadow of early morning and still have plenty of time to set up camp at Squaw Flat Campground in The Needles and then return late in the afternoon to photograph North Six-shooter Peak.

The Needles (23)

The Vista: Far from the life-sustaining waters of the Colorado River, The Needles' desolate mesas and canyons offered few dependable water sources. Tucked beneath the rimrock, Cave Spring could hardly be called an oasis in any desert, yet it offered shade, shelter, and reliable water for ancestral Puebloans from A.D. 900 to 1250. Using natural pigments, they spray painted the outlines of their hands and brushstroked stylized hands resembling *Madi*—East Indian hand tattoos—on the fire-blackened walls of Cave Spring. Some archaeologists believe hands represent personal signatures or were used to call power from a sacred site. The bird pictograph at Cave Spring suggests it was a sacred area. Archaeologist Polly Schaafsma wrote: "Bird symbolism is prevalent in shamanic symbolism throughout the world. Shamans often claim to be able to engage in flights in which the soul, when it leaves the body, takes the form of a bird."

Stockmen who ran cattle in the area during the 1800s needed 200 acres of high desert to graze and feed a cow and a calf for one year. They also needed dependable drinking water for cowboys and their remuda of horses. Cave Spring offered fresh water and shelter for the Scorup–Summerville Cattle Company that ran upward of 10,000 cattle in the remote slickrock country. Cave Spring served as a dependable line camp for cave-dwelling cowboys from the late 1800s to 1975. Remnants of their tough, colorful heyday can still be seen at this rustic outpost.

During my most recent visit to Canyonlands, I was drawn to the area's pictographs and petroglyphs, but The Needles is a magnet for photographers, hikers, and four-wheel-drive enthusiasts. When Professor John S. Newberry first saw the "forest" of white and brown Cedar Mesa Sandstone spires on August 23, 1859, he wrote: "Scattered over the plain were thousands of fantastically

Directions: From Moab, Utah, drive 40 miles south on US 191 to the junction of UT 211 (14 miles north of Monticello). Turn left (west) on UT 211, and drive 35 miles to The Needles Visitor Center.

The Hikes: ½-mile Cave Springs Loop Trail, ½-mile Pothole Point Trail, 2½-mile Slickrock Foot Trail, 6-mile Chesler Park View Point, 7½-mile Big Springs Canyon Trail, 11-mile Druid Arch Trail, 11-mile Confluence Overlook Trail, and others

Natural Hazards: Heat during summer; lightning and flash floods during monsoons; ice and snow during winter

Contact: Phone 435-259-4711, or visit www.nps.gov/cany/needles

Entrance Fee: $10 per vehicle for seven days or a National Parks Pass

Campground Fee: Squaw Flat, $10 per night; group sites, $3 per night

Backcountry Permits and Fees: Fees vary, depending on the activity. Phone 435-259-4712, or visit www.nps.gov/cany/reserve.

Maps (optional): USGS 7.5-minute maps: The Loop, Druid Arch, and North Sixshooter Peak, Utah

Neighboring Camera Stops: The Maze, phone 435-259-2652, or visit www.nps.gov/cany/maze; Horseshoe Canyon, phone 435-259-2652, or visit www.nps.gov/cany/horseshoe

Season: All year

Cave Springs hand pictograph, The Needles, Canyonlands National Park

Colorado River Rock Art (24)

The Vista: Renowned for its majestic river canyons, colorful history of pioneer river runners and photographers, and the uranium rush of the 1960s, the Colorado River near Moab, Utah, proffers a diverse array of rock art that has gone largely unnoticed except by vandals, zealots, and thieves bent on destroying, erasing, or stealing these irreplaceable cultural treasures with gunfire, spray paint, graffiti, climbers chalk, sledgehammers, chisels, and crowbars. Dating far beyond the region's written or oral history, the wealth of the sacred etchings and paintings found along the course of the Colorado River and the Old Spanish Trail include: haunting shamans and spirit helpers of Archaic hunters and gatherers that date back 3,000 to 4,000 years; sandal tracks, ceremonial dancers, and anthropomorphs of ancestral Puebloans that date between A.D. 900 and 1250; and horned men and bighorn sheep of the Mukwic[1] (ancestral Ute and Paiute) that date back to the same era; and historic horseback hunting scenes of the Paiute, Ute, and Navajo that date between A.D. 1250 and the late 1800s.

Few of these scenes are thought to be as significant as the Birthing Scene near Kane Creek at Kings Bottom on the Colorado River. Except for Native peoples who can still trace their lineage directly back to sacred rock drawings and paintings,

formed buttes . . . pyramids, domes, towers, columns, spires, of every conceivable form and size . . . they extend like a belt of timber for a distance of several miles. Nothing in nature or in art offers a parallel to these singular objects."

Photography: Cave Spring is only one of many enticing destinations for photographers in The Needles. A variety of trails lead to the multicolored fins and spires of Chesler Park, the double span of 390-foot-tall Druid Arch, the 4,800-foot (±) Confluence Overlook of the Green and Colorado Rivers, and other destinations that you can spend a season photographing in this slickrock wilderness. The 6.4-mile Scenic Drive to 4,800-foot (±) Big Spring Canyon Overlook is an ideal spot during late afternoon to photograph the mushroom-shaped Navajo sandstone hoodoos, as is Utah 211 east of The Needles Visitor Center, where undeveloped pullouts offer opportunities to photograph 6,374-foot North Six-shooter Peak at twilight.

---

[1] Archaeologists often call the ancestral Ute and Paiute the "Fremont" culture or people, but it is a disparaging term for traditional Native peoples to have their ancestors named after John C. Fremont because they believe his 1850s exploration led to their cultural demise.

Directions: From Main Street and Kane Creek Boulevard in Moab, Utah, drive 2 miles west on Kane Creek Road to the Moonflower Canyon petroglyphs. Drive 3 miles farther on the dirt road until you reach an unmarked pullout on the right. The "Birthing Scene Rock Art Panel" is located 25 yards below the road on a large boulder.

The Hikes: Roadside walks

Natural Hazards: Heat during summer; lightning and flash floods during monsoons

Contact: Discover Moab, phone 800-635-6622, or visit www.discovermoab.com

Entrance Fee: No fee

Map (optional): USGS 7.5-minute map: Moab, Utah

Guide: Canyonlands Natural History Association, phone 800-840-8978, or visit www.cnha.org to order a copy of *Into the Mystery: A Driving Tour of Moab Area Petroglyphs and Pictographs* by Janet Lowe

Neighboring Camera Stops: Arches National Park

Season: All year

desert varnish. Direct early-morning and late-afternoon light are best, but late to midafternoon also works well in shadowed light.

Use Extreme Caution: Tread gently. Remember where you are, and respect what these ancient paintings and etchings represent. Hand oils and chalk are destructive, so don't touch or try to "enhance" any pictographs or petroglyphs. Share your images, and enlighten and educate others to the fragile nature of the West's disappearing rock art.

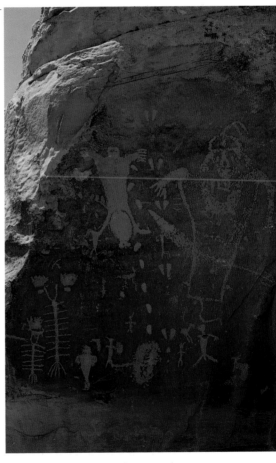

archaeologists' interpretations of pictographs and petroglyphs are, at best, educated guesses. Some believe the Birthing Scene represents a mother giving birth to a child while the shaman or healer sings and prays for the mother in childbirth.

This is truly a miraculous scene to contemplate near the Colorado River in an area where virtually every other rock art site has suffered at the hands of modern man.

Photography: Pictographs are painted onto smooth walls with natural pigments and dyes. Petroglyphs are pecked into

Birthing scene petroglyph, Kings Bottom, Colorado River

VIII. Arches National Park

The Story Behind the Scenery: Located north of Canyonland's National Park in the Y between the Green and Colorado Rivers, Arches National Park is surrounded by the big western scenery of the 12,721-foot La Sal Mountains to the southeast, the San Rafael Desert to the west, and the Roan and Book Cliffs to the north. A harsh, high, roseate desert that's blistering hot in the summer and freezing cold in the winter, Arches is one of the most scenic and renowned landscapes in the United States. Only Navajoland's Monument Valley, 150 miles south, rivals it. Overlaying an underground seabed of salt 300 million years old, the 300-foot-thick Entrada sandstone formation buckled, faulted, and thrust upward, molding the earth's crust into fins, domes, spires, and canyons. One hundred million years of wind, water, ice, and freeze-thaw erosion sculpted a mesmerizing landscape found nowhere else in the world. More than 2,000 arches have been recorded in Arches National Park, from 3-foot-wide "windows" to the 306-foot span of Landscape Arch. Devoid of life at first glance, the heart of this barren, mile-high slickrock desert is home to 65 species of mammals, including desert bighorn sheep, mule deer, jackrabbits, and coyotes; 190 species of birds, including golden eagles, pinyon jays, and canyon wrens; and 22 species of reptiles, including the collared and western whiptail lizards.

In his 1964 book, *Standing Up Country*, C. Gregory Crampton wrote: "There is as much country standing up as there is laying down." There are few bet-

ter examples of Canyon Country's contrary characteristic than Delicate Arch. Backdropped by the snow-covered peaks of the La Sal Mountains, Delicate Arch

stands on a pink bluff 500 feet above Salt Wash, Cash Valley Wash, and Winter Camp Wash. When Moab cowboys first laid eyes on Delicate Arch while tracking maverick cattle across the rimrock during the 1880s, they called it the "Schoolmarm's Bloomers" and the "Chaps." One can only speculate how the Mukwic and Anaasází, and later the Paiute, Ute, and Navajo, envisioned the fragile window of stone that would become the license plate icon for the state of Utah.

Bypassed by the 1830s Old Spanish Trail, the 1859 Macomb Survey, and the 1869 and 1871–72 Powell Expeditions down the Green and Colorado Rivers, the

Tower of Babel, Arches National Park

stunning scenery of Arches lured few outsiders until Civil War veteran John Wesley Wolfe built a chinked log cabin on Salt Wash and ramrodded the Bar-DX Ranch near the foot of Delicate Arch in 1888. Until Wolfe sold out his frontier homestead in 1910, he had the run of Arches to himself. So did New York photographer Harry Reid. When Reid came calling in 1935, cowboys told him: "They wa'ant nothin' out there. Jest a lot of holes in rocks." That's pretty much the way Edward Abbey found Arches when he drove the dirt road from the potash-and-cattle boomtown Mormon settlement of Moab across the slickrock to a government trailer at the foot of Balanced Rock a half century ago. In his seminal 1968 book, *Desert Solitaire: A Season in the Wilderness,* Abbey ignited the environmental movement with passionate and eloquent prose that could not be denied: "Standing there, gaping at this monstrous and inhuman spectacle of rock and cloud and sky and space, I feel a ridiculous greed and possessiveness come over me. I want to know it all, possess it all, embrace the entire scene intimately, deeply, totally. . . . [A]t least there's nothing else, no one human, to dispute possession with me."

Times changed. On January 20, 1969, President Lyndon B. Johnson established Arches National Park, and people from all walks of life and all parts of the globe beat a path to this remote corner of Utah to see its postcard scenic wonders.

First Photographed: Timothy H. O'Sullivan photographed an area distant from Devils Garden called Witches Rocks in

---

Directions: From Moab, Utah, drive 5 miles north on US 191 to the Arches Visitor Center

The Drive: From the visitor center, $22\frac{1}{2}$ miles of paved Scenic Drive loops through the park

Natural Hazards: Traffic and heat during summer; lightning and flash floods during monsoons; ice and snow during winter

Contact: Phone 435-719-2299, or visit www.nps.gov/arch

Entrance Fee: $10 per vehicle for seven days or a National Parks Pass

Campground: Devils Campground, $10 per night. For reservations, phone 877-444-6777, or visit www.reserve usa.com.

Hiking Permits Required: For day use of the Fiery Furnace and all overnight backpacking

Maps (optional): USGS 7.5-minute maps: Moab, The Windows Section, Mollie Hogans, Big Bend, and Klondike Bluffs, Utah

Season: All year

Canyonlands Natural History Association: Phone 800-840-8978, or visit www .cnha.org

Discover Moab: Phone 800-635-6622, or visit www.discovermoab.com

Guides: *Arches of Arches National Park: A Comprehensive Study* by J. Edward McCarrick, and *Desert Rock: A Climber's Guide to the Canyon Country of the American Southwest Desert* by Erick Bjørnstad. Contact Back of Beyond Books, 800-700-2859, or visit www .backofbeyondbooks.com. Or stop in and browse at 83 North Main Street, Moab, UT 84532.

Nefertiti's Head, Arches National Park

Echo, Utah, in 1869 and later photographed Green River, Utah, in 1874. O'Sullivan's photographs are reproduced in Joel Snyder's 1981 book, *American Frontiers*. The first-published photograph of the Moab area's rock trusses may have been taken by Stuart M. Young. Young's photograph of the Pritchett Valley Bridge (49 feet tall, 122-foot span), illustrates Byron Cummings's February 1910 *National Geographic* magazine article, "The Great Natural Bridges of Utah."

Photography: Arches National Park is much like Bryce Canyon National Park. The formations are so colorful and alluring that it's difficult to take a bad photograph in ideal light. It's also so small and accessible, and has been photographed by so many different photographers, that it's difficult to take an original image unless you listen to your heart and seek your own vision that stands apart from the familiar scenes photographers continue to photocopy.

Park Avenue & Courthouse Towers (25)

The Vista: Seen from the 4,600-foot (±) Park Avenue Viewpoint, the scenery here defies your expectations of what you thought you'd see in landscape renowned for its arches and flying buttresses of pink and golden stone. Majestic walls and towering monuments that bear striking resemblances to the mesas, buttes, and spires of Monument Valley turn your head in every direction. Left (west) of the viewpoint, you'll see 4,982-foot Courthouse Towers and the unmistakable skyline profile of Nefertiti's head. To the right (east), you'll see the candlestick formations of the Candelabrum. Lured by the challenges of climbing virgin walls of Entrada and Navajo sandstone, rock climbers named three of Candelabrum's formations when they first climbed them in 1986 and 1987: Hall of Flame, A Company of Candles, and Play With Fire. Out of sight high above the viewpoint is Queen Victoria. Named for the English monarch who reigned from 1837 to 1901, the name reflects the influences of Euro-American pioneers who settled the area during the 1800s.

The scenery at the 4,200-foot (±) Courthouse Towers Viewpoint a mile north is no less stunning. Looming overhead is the Organ (500 feet tall), and due north is the 4,537-foot Tower of Babel (550 feet tall). Across the highway to the west is Sheep Rock (440 feet tall), the narrowest finger of rock in Arches, and to the southwest are the Three Gossips (280 feet tall). The Park Avenue and Courthouse Towers area is wonderful to photograph, but it's only one of six geologically distinct scenic sections of Arches National Park that include the Windows, Delicate Arch, Fiery Furnace, Devils Garden, and Klondike Bluffs.

Photography: You can easily spend two days photographing the Park Avenue and Courthouse Towers area. Park Avenue and Courthouse Towers are best photographed between late afternoon and twilight. The Three Gossips and Sheep Rock are best photographed between first light and early morning.

The Windows (26)

The Vista: Standing at the gateway to The Windows is a pedestal of stone called Balanced Rock. Edward Abbey drew inspiration from the pygmy forest of piñon and juniper that surrounds the precariously-perched stone during his literary tenure at Arches. A mile beyond is the Garden of Eden. Its two most recognizable formations are 5,653-foot Elephant Butte (250 feet tall) and Owl Rock (100 feet tall). In the traditional beliefs of some Native peoples, the owl is the harbinger of death; though in the golden light of sunset, Owl Rock looks like a beacon of good fortune. Drive a mile and a half farther, and you'll reach the pullouts and trailheads to the Windows. Follow the Windows Loop Trail, and you'll see Turret Arch. Standing 64 feet high and spanning 39 feet, Turret Arch is, as one anonymous early writer wrote, "a great spear-headed tower. . . . [T]he arch itself is shaped something like a keyhole of Brobdingnagian proportions." The 51-foot-high, 93-foot span of the North Window and the 66-foot-high, 105-foot span of the South Window form The Windows. One of the most popular and photocopied

---

Directions: From the Arches Visitor Center, drive 2 miles to the Park Avenue Viewpoint, then 1 mile north to the Courthouse Towers Viewpoint
The Hike: Roadside strolls, and the 1-mile Park Avenue Trail (320-foot descent) to the Scenic Drive at the Courthouse Towers Viewpoint
Neighboring Camera Stops: The Windows
Map (optional): The Windows Section, Utah

Directions: From the Arches Visitor Center, drive 9.2 miles to the turnoff for The Windows (7.2 miles from the Park Avenue viewpoint), then 2.5 miles farther to The Windows trailhead
The Hikes: Roadside strolls, ¾-mile Double Arch Trail, and 1-mile Windows Loop Trail
Neighboring Camera Stops: Delicate Arch
Map (optional): The Windows Section, Utah

Tree at twilight, The Windows, Arches National Park

compositions of Arches National Park is the sunrise photograph of Turret Arch framed by the orange walls of the North Window. Nearby Double Arch on the southern rim of Elephant Butte is, in my opinion, one of the most remarkable arches in the park. The largest span of the 105-foot-high Double Arch measures 163 feet across, and the smaller span measures 60 feet across. Scramble up the sand spit, and view the blue skies through double windows of brown stone.

Photography: Double Arch and The Windows are best photographed in early morning, and Turret Arch is best photographed in late afternoon. Photographing The Windows or Turret Arch during busy summer months can be difficult because many visitors watch the sun rise and set from perches beneath these spans.

Delicate Arch (27)

The Vista: Standing 45 feet tall, and 33 feet wide, Delicate Arch has for years offered a stone picture frame for photographers using the La Sal Mountains as their backdrop. The 310-foot span of Kolob Arch in Zion National Park, and the 200-foot span of Wrather Arch in Paria Canyon, Vermilion Cliffs National Monument, dwarf Delicate Arch. The needle-

Directions: From the Arches Visitor Center, drive 11.7 miles the Delicate Arch turnoff (2.5 miles from the Windows turnoff), then 1.2 miles farther to the Delicate Arch Trailhead

The Hike: 1½-mile Delicate Arch Trail (480-foot climb, across the slickrock)

Neighboring Camera Stops: Wolfe Ranch petroglyphs

Maps (optional): The Windows Section and Big Bend, Utah

thin 306-foot span of Landscape Arch in Devils Garden is narrower then all of them at a mere 6 feet thick. But no other arch I've seen compares to the fragile beauty of Delicate Arch. It is the arch against which all other arches and natural bridges are compared. Edward Abbey was right when he wrote: "After Delicate Arch the others are anticlimactic."

Take a seat on the stone bench overlooking 4,800-foot (±) Delicate Arch, and watch the setting sun paint this exquisite skylight with subtle brushstrokes of yellow, orange, and pink. Or scurry across the slickrock, and scramble up the aerie to the southwest for a raptor's view of Delicate Arch standing at the head of the line of domes on the ridge behind it. Both will leave you with views that you won't soon forget.

Photography: Regardless of your point of view, Delicate Arch is extremely difficult to photograph during busy summer months. Many visitors pay homage at the foot of this storied landmark until the last glimmer of light dances from heavenly night skies.

Delicate Arch, Arches National Park

Fiery Furnace (28)

Spire, Fiery Furnace, Arches National Park

The Vista: Named for both its incandescent glow at sunset and its hellish summer heat, the Fiery Furnace is located on the southern end of Devils Garden. It has the kind of look-alike terrain that spooks many hikers with doubts of the *no way out, dead end, enter at your own risk, what are we doing here* kind. Described as "a mazelike labyrinth of narrow sandstone canyons," no other area in Arches National Park is billed as difficult, confusing, and dangerous to explore alone as the Fiery Furnace. Probe the slickrock corridors, cul de sacs, pour offs, and box canyons alone, and you may feel: *Man*

Directions: From the Arches Visitor Center, drive 14.5 miles to the Fiery Furnace Viewpoint (2.5 miles from the Delicate Arch turnoff)

The Hike: Roadside stroll or 1 to 2 miles (depending on your route) of trailless canyoneering through an exciting network of slickrock passages, cracks, ledges, canyons, and drop-offs

Caution: If you're hiking alone, stop every few minutes to take a mental picture of your route; if you have doubts about the route ahead, retrace your footsteps; and don't climb down anything you don't think you can safely climb back up

Day Use Permit and Fee: $2 per person. Ranger guided walks are $8 per person and $4 per child (6 to 12 years old).

Neighboring Camera Stops: Devils Garden

Maps (optional): The Windows Section, and Mollie Hogans, Utah

---

does not belong here. Surprise Arch is one of many enticements to explore Fiery Furnace's otherworldly terrain alone or in the company of a guide. Discovered by park rangers in 1963, Surprise Arch is 55 feet high and spans 63 feet.

This is an enchanting and exciting—if a bit unnerving—place to photograph alone during summer monsoons when the gods of lightning, flash floods, and rockfall rule this hidden landscape. Thunder booming and echoing through the Fiery Furnace's secret chambers can humble you.

Photography: You can photograph its landmark pinnacles from the 4,800-foot (±) Fiery Furnace Viewpoint between late afternoon and sunset, or you can venture into the Fiery Furnace and photograph its corridors of stone midmorning and midafternoon.

Devils Garden (29)

The Vista: Hungarian miner Alexander Ringhoffer is credited with "discovering" Arches in 1922 while prospecting the Klondike Bluffs area 5 miles west of Devils Garden. The 5,298-foot Klondike Bluffs takes its name from the 1890s Klondike Gold Rush when 30,000 prospectors pulled $22 million worth of gold out of Bonanza Creek in the Yukon Territories. Ringhoffer must have seen something other than "gold in them thar' hills" when he called Klondike Bluffs "Devils Garden." Park officials apparently agreed, for they later switched the name to describe the area from Klondike Bluffs to Devils Garden. Blind alleys and narrow box canyons pinched between soaring fins and sheer walls formed "slickrock corrals" that cowboys used during the 1880s to pen cattle.

Arches abound throughout Devils Garden. Easiest to reach is Skyline Arch; 45 feet high, it spans 69 feet and can be photographed between late afternoon and twilight from a roadside pullout. Sand Dune Arch, hidden in the cul de sac of a narrow canyon, can be reached via a short walk

Fins, Devils Garden, Arches National Park

Directions: From the Arches Visitor Center, drive 17.7 miles to the Devils Garden Trailhead (2.5 miles from the Fiery Furnace turnoff)
The Hikes: 1½ miles round-trip to Landscape Arch, 4 miles round-trip to Double O Arch, and 5 miles round-trip to Dark Angel
Neighboring Camera Stops: Fiery Furnace and Klondike Bluffs. (I haven't been to Klondike Bluffs, so I can't describe them from firsthand experience).
Maps (optional): Mollie Hogans and Klondike Bluffs, Utah

and sand slog and is best photographed during the refracted light of midmorning and midafternoon. Landscape Arch, Double O Arch, and Dark Angel are clustered together in narrow canyons near the north end of Devils Garden and are reached via easy hikes leading from the 5,200-foot (±) Devils Garden Trailhead. Spanning 306 feet, Landscape Arch is best photographed between sunrise and early morning, as is Double O Arch. Its largest O spans 71 feet and its smaller O spans 21 feet.

Photography: If you're drawn to this whimsical landscape for its namesake arches, you will be captivated by the pink light of dawn and the purple glow of twilight washing across the elegant walls and fins of Devils Garden. Like Park Avenue and Courthouse Towers, you can easily spend two days photographing here. You can photograph Devils Garden at sunrise and sunset by scrambling up the slickrock encircling the campground, or you can pick your spot, hike or drive, and wait for magic hour to ignite the rainbows of stone in your viewfinder.

IX. Black Canyon of the Gunnison National Park

The Vista: Black Canyon of the Gunnison is a deep, dark, somber gorge that slashes across the landscape from the "Roof of the Rocky Mountains" to the Colorado Plateau. Seen from the 8,289-foot South Rim, it appears to have few rivals in the West. Black Canyon is 53 miles long and 1,725 feet deep at its narrowest and most profound point, but it is dwarfed by the Grand Canyon and its tributaries of Kanab Creek Canyon and the Little Colorado River Gorge. A daunting sight to behold nonetheless, Black Canyon was largely avoided by the Taviwach band of Ute who first inhabited the area around A.D. 1000. The Taviwach called the canyon *Unaweap*, "the place of high rocks and much water," and, according to historian Elaine Hale Jones, "believed that if anyone attempted to follow the [Gunnison] River through the dark chasm . . . [they] would never return alive." For good reason. Unaweap Cañon carried roaring snowmelt from the 14,000-foot-high Continental Divide through a river gorge five times steeper than the Grand Canyon of the Colorado River. Skirted on the west by the 1776 Domínguez and Escalante Expedition, Black Canyon was "discovered" in 1809 by mountain men and trappers James Workman and Samuel Spencer. When the Hayden Survey later visited the North Rim of the Black Canyon in 1874, they were so inspired by the view that they named it the "Grand Cañon of the Gunnison."

The first non-Indians to actually descend into Black Canyon were surveyors for the 1882 Denver and Rio Grand Railroad expedition. But after two months of struggling down the icy gorge with rods and chains, they realized that the idea of building a railroad through the chasm was preposterous. In 1900, under the leadership of William H. Torrence, a half-starved, five-man expedition gave up at the Falls of Sorrows after a month of trying to run the Gunnison River in two canvas boats. But they still had to escape Black Canyon's deadly grip. In a *Colorado Magazine* article, Richard G. Beidleman wrote: "They roped together and, using their spike-shod transit tripod legs as alpenstocks, they slowly made their precarious way, one after another, up the canyon wall. By noon, they had scaled a thousand feet. In the afternoon one of the company could hardly be restrained from jumping into the chasm. Finally, at 3:30 in the afternoon the rim was reached. The men were exhausted, covered with dust, parched, hands cut, lips swollen, eyes bloodshot. Even then, they were still in wild, uninhabited country and had to hike fifteen miles before they encountered William McMillen's ranch."

Incredibly, Torrence returned to Black Canyon in 1901 with Geological Survey hydrographer A. Lincoln Fellows with plans to survey it for the proposed Gunnison River diversion project. Determined to swim any part of the river that couldn't be boated, Torrence and Fellows survived their adventure by bulldogging a bighorn sheep and killing it with a hunting knife. They succeeded in completing their survey in seven days.

Black Canyon of the Gunnison eventu-

Chasm view, Black Canyon of the Gunnison National Park

ally drew the attention of famed Grand Canyon photographers and explorers Emery and Ellsworth Kolb. During the summer of 1916, two years after photo-graphing and taking the first motion pictures of their Grand Canyon river expedition from Green River, Wyoming, to the Gulf of California, they tried their luck at running Black Canyon. But the Kolb brothers wrecked their boat in the gorge, and, according to Beidleman, they "only saved their lives by scaling 1700-foot cliffs." President Herbert Hoover established Gunnison National Monument on March 2, 1933. It became a national park in 1999.

First Photographed: In all likelihood, members of the 1874 Hayden Survey first photographed the Grand Cañon of the Gunnison from the North Rim, though it's not widely known if William Henry Jackson took the photographs or not. The inner canyon was first photographed by members of the five-man Torrance expedition during September 1900. Several of these photographs illustrate Richard D. Beidleman's July 1959 *Colorado Magazine* article, "The Gunnison River Diversion Project."

Photography: The views from the South Rim's scenic vistas are head-spinning. Like many scenic drives, you get the feeling that you're driving through a postcard. To photograph the gorge from below—and taste the adventure of Torrence, Fellows, and the Kolbs—you have to descend to the Gunnsion River. I skied down—and clawed up—the Tomichi Route.

Directions: From Montrose, Colorado, drive 8.2 miles east on US 50 to the junction of CO 347. Drive 7 miles north on CO 347 to the South Rim Visitor Center.

The Drive: From the visitor center, the paved 7-mile South Rim Road Drive leads to 8,289-foot High Point on its west end. The scenic viewpoints en route include Gunnison Point, Pulpit Rock Overlook, Cross Fissures View, Chasm View, Painted Wall View, and Sunset Point.

The Hikes: Short rim trails (¼ mile to ⁴/₁₀ miles round-trip) lead to spectacular vistas such as Rock Point, Devils Lookout, Cedar Point, Dragon Point, and Warner Point. Incredibly steep rim-to-river routes, such as the South Rim's 1-mile Gunnison Point (1,800-foot vertical drop) and 2-mile Warner Point (2,660-foot vertical drop), and the North Rim's 1¾-mile S.O.B Draw (1,800-foot vertical drop), 1-mile Long Draw (1,800-foot vertical drop), and 1-mile Slide Draw (1,620-foot vertical drop) lead to the banks of the Gunnison River. The 1-mile-long Tomichi Route, arguably one of the steepest canyon "trails" in the United States this side of the Grand Canyon's Lava Falls Trail, drops 1,960 vertical feet from the South Rim's 8,286-foot Tomichi Point to the Gunnison River. Travel light, and insure your knees with Lloyd's of London beforehand.

Natural Hazards: Lightning at the scenic viewpoints, loose rock and talus on steep rim-to-river descents, and exhaustion on river-to-rim ascents

Contact: Phone 970-249-1914, or visit www.nps.gov/blca

Entrance Fee: $8 per vehicle for seven days or a National Parks Pass

Campground Fee: South Rim Campground, $10 per night

Backcountry Permit: Check the website for the latest information.

Map (optional): USGS 7.5-minute map: Grizzly Ridge, Colorado

Neighboring Camera Stops: Mesa Verde National Park, Colorado

Season: Spring through fall

Western National Parks Association: Visit www.wnpa.org

Suggested Reading

Abbey, Edward. *Slickrock: Endangered Canyons of the Southwest* (photographs and commentary by Philip Hyde), cloth. New York: Sierra Club/Charles Scribner's Sons, 1971.

Annerino, John. *Grand Canyon Wild: A Photographic Journey* (photographs by the author), cloth. Woodstock, VT: Countryman Press, 2004.

——. *People of Legend: Native Americans of the Southwest* (photographs by the author), cloth. San Francisco: Sierra Club Books, 1996.

——. "Navajo Mountain" in *Hiking the Southwest* by Dave Ganci (pps. 192–96). San Francisco: Sierra Club Books, 1983.

Babbitt, James E. *Rainbow Trails: Early Day Adventures in Rainbow Bridge Country.* Page, AZ: Glen Canyon Natural History Association, 1990.

Bandelier, Adolf F. *The Delight Makers* (with photographs by Chas F. Lummis and Frederick C. Hicks), cloth, 2nd edition. New York: Dodd, Mead and Company, 1916. First edition 1890.

Beidleman, Richard G. "The Gunnison River Diversion Project, Exploration of the Black Canyon," Part I. *The Colorado Magazine,* State Historical Society of Colorado, Vol. XXXVI, No. 3 (July 1959): 187–201.

Breed, Jack. "First Motor Sortie in Escalante Land" (photographs by the author). *National Geographic,* Vol. XCVI, No. 3 (September 1949): 367–404.

Crawford, J. L. *Zion Album: A Nostalgic History of Zion Canyon* (historic, hand-colored lantern slides by Randall Jones, Homer Jones, Angus M. Woodbury, E. T. Scoyen, Arden Schiefer, Harold Russell, and others). Springdale, UT: Zion Natural History Association, 1986.

Cummings, Byron. "The Great Natural Bridges of Utah" (photographs by Stuart M. Young). *National Geographic,* Vol. 21, no. 2 (February 1910): 157–170.

Darrah, William Culp. "Beaman, Fennemore, Hillers, Dellenbaugh, Johnson and Hattan." In "The Exploration of the Colorado River and the High Plateaus of Utah by the Second Powell Expedition of 1871–72." *Utah Historical Quarterly,* Vols. XVI-XVII (1948–49): 491–503.

Dellenbaugh, Frederick S. *A Canyon Voyage: The Narrative of the Second Powell Expedition Down the Green-Colorado River from Wyoming, and the Exploration on Land, in the years 1871 and 1872.* New York and London: G. P. Putnam's Sons, 1908.

——. *Romance of the Colorado River: The Story of its Discovery in 1540, With an Account of the Later Explorations, and with Special References to the Voyages of Powell Through the Line of Great Canyons.* New York and London: G. P. Putnam's Sons, 1902.

Fowler, Don D., editor. *"Photographed All the Best Scenery," Jack Hillers' Diary of the Powell Expeditions, 1871–1875.* Salt Lake City: University of Utah Press, 1972.

——. *Myself in the Water: The Western*

Photographs of John K. Hillers. Washington, DC and London: Smithsonian Institution, 1989.

Hassel, Hank. *Rainbow Bridge: An Illustrated History* (line drawings and maps by R. Sean Evans). Logan: Utah State University Press, 1999.

Hughes, Jim. *The Birth of a Century: Early Color Photographs of America* (photographs by William Henry Jackson and The Detroit Photographic Company), cloth. London and New York: Tauris Parke Books, 1994.

Jackson, William Henry. *Time Exposure: The Autobiography of William Henry Jackson.* New York: G. P. Putnam's Sons, 1940.

———. "Ancient Ruins in Southwestern Colorado" in *Eighth Annual Report of the United States Geological and Geographical Survey of the Territories, Embracing Colorado and Parts of Adjacent Territories; Being a Report of Progress of the Exploration for the Year 1874* by F. V. Hayden. Washington, DC: Government Printing Office, 1876.

Kelly, Charles. "The Mysterious "D. Julien." Utah Historical Quarterly. Vol. 6, No. 3 (July 1933): 83–88.

Kolb, E. L. *Through the Grand Canyon from Wyoming to Mexico.* New York: MacMillan Company, 1914.

Lummis, Charles F. *The Land of Poco Tiempo* (photographs by the author), cloth, 2nd edition. New York: Charles Scriber's Sons, 1928. First edition 1893.

McCarrick, J. Edward. *The Arches of Arches National Park: A Comprehensive Study.* Orem, UT: Mainstay Publishing, 1988.

Nichols, Tad. *Glen Canyon: Images of the Lost World* (photographs by the author), cloth. Santa Fe: Museum of New Mexico Press, 1999.

O'Sullivan, Timothy H. *Wheeler's Photographic Survey of the American West, 1871–1873.* New York: Dover, 1983.

Porter, Eliot. *The Place No One Knew: Glen Canyon on the Colorado* (photographs by the author, edited by David Brower), cloth. San Francisco: Sierra Club Books, 1963.

Powell, J. W. *Exploration of the Colorado River of the West and its Tributaries, Explored in 1869, 1870, 1871, and 1872.* Washington, DC: Government Printing Office, 1875.

Roosevelt, Theodore. *A Book-Lover's Holidays in the Open.* New York: Charles Scribner's Sons, 1916.

Stephens, Hal G., and Eugene M. Shoemaker (historical photographs by E. O. Beaman and John K. "Jack" Hillers). *In the Footsteps of John Wesley Powell: An Album of Comparative Photographs of the Green and Colorado Rivers, 1871–72 and 1968.* Boulder and Denver, CO: Johnson Books and The Powell Society, 1967.

Thompson, Almon Harris. "Diary of Almon Harris Thompson: Geographer, Explorations of the Colorado River of the West and Its Tributaries, 1871–1875." *Utah State Historical Quarterly,* Vol. VII, Nos. 1, 2, and 3 (January, April, and July 1939): 1–140.

Trip & Expedition Planner

Photography

Film: For discounted prices on bricks of Fuji Velvia and Provia, and air courier shipments, phone B&H Photo at 800-947-1186, or visit www.bhphoto.com.

Processing: Fuji Color Processing; phone 866-890-3854, ext. 4755, or visit www.fujifilm.com.

Thors Hammer, Bryce Canyon National Park

Digital Compact Flash Cards: For Lexar Media, visit www.lexarmedia.com; for SanDisk Extreme, visit www.sandisk.com.

Image Rescue: Lexar Media, visit www.lexarmedia.com.

Camera Developing: Visit www.digitalcameradeveloping.com.

Workshops, Lectures, Seminars: International Center of Photography, phone 212-857-0001, or visit www.icp.org.

National Parks, Monuments, and Recreation Areas

Entrance Fees: Save on entrance fees by purchasing a $50 National Parks Pass on your next visit to a national park, monument, or recreation area; phone 888-GO-PARKS, or visit www.nps.gov.

Camping and Backcountry Permits: Fees for camping and backcountry use vary from park to park. Refer to each listing in this guide, or visit www.nps.gov.

Campground Reservations: Phone 800-365-CAMP, or visit www.reservations.nps.gov.

Or phone 877-444-6777, or visit www.reservusa.com.

Lodging at Zion and Bryce Canyon: Phone 888-297-2757, or visit www.xanterra.com

Books and Guides

By Foot, Raft, Rope, and Pickup Truck

Annerino, John. *Canyon Country: A Photographic Journey.* Woodstock, VT: Countryman Press, 2005. Phone 802-457-4826, or visit www.countryman press.com.

———. *The Photographer's Guide to the Grand Canyon.* Woodstock, VT: Countryman Press, 2005. Phone 802-457-4826, or visit www.countryman press.com.

———. *Canyons of the Southwest: A Tour of the Great Canyon Country from Colorado to Northern Mexico.* San Francisco: Sierra Club Books, 1993. University of Arizona Press paperback edition, 2000. Phone 800-426-3797, or visit www.uapress.arizona.edu.

———. "Training, Gear, Hiking, Water, Hazards, and Emergency Evacuation" in *Hiking the Grand Canyon.* San Francisco: Sierra Club Books, 1986. Revised edition 1993, new 3rd edition 2006. Phone 800-777-4726, or visit www.sierraclub.org/books.

Bjørnstead, Eric. *Desert Rock: A Climber's Guide to the Canyon Country of the American Southwest Desert.* Denver: Chockstone Press, 1988. Phone 303-377-1970.

Coronella, Mike, and Joe Mitchell. *The Hayduke Trail.* Salt Lake City: University of Utah Press, 2005. Visit www .uofupress.com.

Lowe, Janet. *Into the Mystery: A Driving Tour of Moab Area Petroglyphs and Pictographs.* Moab, UT: Canyonlands Natural History Association, 2000. Phone 800-840-8978, or visit www .cnha.org.

On the River and Lake

Belknap, Bill, and Buzz Belknap. *Canyonlands River Guide: Westwater, Lake Powell, Canyonlands National Park.* Boulder City, NV: Westwater Books, 1974. Phone 800-628-1326.

Jones, Stan. *Stan Jones' Lake Powell Country and Glen Canyon National Recreation Area in Arizona and Utah* (map and sketches by the author). Page, AZ: Sun Country Publications, 1980. Write Stan Jones, P.O. Box 955, Page, AZ 86040.

Poisonous Bites and Stings

Smith, Robert L., (illustrated by Joel Floyd). *Venomous Animals of Arizona.* Tucson: University of Arizona, College of Agriculture, 1982. Phone 877-763-5315, or visit www.cals.arizona.edu/ pub.

Maps

Driving

National Park Maps: Available free at National Park entrance stations, these U.S. Geological Survey 1:100,000 scale color maps are the handiest references for visiting established scenic vistas and popular points of interest. Washington, DC: U.S. Government Printing Office, 2003, (most current date). Visit www.nps.gov.

Guide to Indian Country: This is the best, most detailed and accurate road and highway map to the Colorado Plateau and Four Corners region. Los Angeles: Automobile Club of Southern California, 1996. Phone 520-622-1999, or visit www .wnpa.org, (Western National Parks Association).

Hiking

U.S. Geological Survey Topographical Maps: The 7.5-minute quadrangles and 1 x 2 Degree Series maps listed at the end of each photo destination can be ordered by visiting www.usgs.gov.

Shuttles

Zion and Bryce Canyon: Between April and October, shuttle buses provide free access between visitor centers, campgrounds, scenic vistas, and popular points of interest. Visit www.nps.gov/zion or www.nps.gov/brca.

Canyoneering

Zion Narrows: Photographers hiking Zion Narrows from top to bottom, call 435-772-1001, or visit www.zionadventures.com for shuttle schedules and fees.

River Expeditions

Green and Colorado Rivers

For a list of Canyonlands river outfitters, contact Moab Area Travel Council at 800-635-6622, or visit www.discovermoab.com. For private river expeditions, visit www.nps.gov/cany/river for permits and fees and http://waterdata.usgs.gov/nwis for river flows.

U.S. Weather Service

Phone 801-524-5133, or visit www.nws.noaa.gov.

Vehicle Survival Kit

Communication: In remote and rugged areas of the Colorado Plateau, a satellite phone is the only dependable form of communication and "trip insurance" for emergencies. Phone 877-977-6305, or visit www.phileasing.com.

For the drive out to remote areas of Grand Staircase–Escalante National Monument, pack a first-aid kit and emergency supplies and take the following precautions:

Itinerary: Leave a detailed map and itinerary with someone you can trust. If you're late calling in or returning home, searchers will know where to look.

Food: In addition to a planned menu, carry nonperishable staples, such as canned food and fruit, dry goods, matches, and stove fuel.

Water: In addition to a 1-gallon per-person-per-day minimum, carry an additional 5-gallon container of water.

Tools: Two spare tires (no donut spares!), a dependable jack, a shovel, a tow rope, fan and alternator belts, fuses, two sources of light, extra batteries, and a tool kit. Important advice: Have your vehicle checked out thoroughly and serviced before you leave home.

Leave No Trace

Leave No Trace/Outdoor Ethics: Phone 800-332-4100, or visit www.lnt.org.